NEW MEXICO, AN INTUITIVE PAINTING RETREAT, AND A
PEACOCK!

BECOMING ZIA

A TALE OF TRANSFORMATION

ZIA POE EUBANKS

Table of Contents

DEDICATION

This book is dedicated to the people in my life who have always loved and accepted me unconditionally. You know who you are! I have been blessed to really be known by some very wonderful, loving and nurturing people. That is a true gift.

Although my grandmother Amy passed away nearly 30 years ago, I have to mention her here. Without her love and acceptance, I don't think I would have survived my childhood. She showed me unconditional love and has been my model for grandmothering. She always had time for me, listened to me, and treated me with respect and value. Something we should all do towards one another. I am honored to have had her in my life, and I wish she was still alive so that she could read this and know how much her loving meant to me.

Writing this book has been a challenge, but one I know I needed to take on. It required vulnerability and honesty, although it didn't seem like I had a choice; the story wanted to be told. I am grateful for Chris Zydel and the wonderful people of the Ghost Ranch in New Mexico for facilitating this transformation. Also, the beautiful women who took this journey with me, and all the lessons I learned from them.

Of course, my girls. Elisha, Zoë, and Isabella, who hold my heart and are my inspiration in so many ways. I love you more than all the stars, trees, leaves, worms, grass blades, ions, atoms, etcetera, etcetera. To infinity x infinity! Is there more love than that?

To my old husband Jeff. No matter what, we had each other's back and understood each other on a level that many wouldn't understand. You never judged me, always accepted me, and rolled with the flow of our mutual craziness like a pro! Thank you! I appreciate you and miss that guy! Especially the one who could fix anything!

To my new husband Jeff. No one can truly understand a Traumatic Brain Injury until they've lived it. And, I don't wish that on anyone! However, yours has opened a new journey for both of us and it has lessons at every turn! You've taught me patience and compassion on an advanced class level, and that is a gift. Your gentle nature shines even brighter now and I never stop learning from you. Life is weird sometimes, but apparently, we are meant to be together! There is a bigger story.

And finally, my mother. I spent my life trying to be something I wasn't to please her. When I finally realized that it was impossible, it was too late. We had danced the dance so long, there was no possible way of changing it up. Unfortunately, she died last year and never knew me. I'm not sure it was even attainable, but I'd always hoped. Today, without the cloud of needing acceptance, I can see her more clearly, and I see her as a human, with her own set of flaws. She loved me the best way she knew how. She was proud of me, even though she didn't fully understand me, or have the capacity. She did her best. But now, I want to set her free. She was amazing in so many ways, and that is what I will remember. She was an artist that had been stifled but it showed up in her life through her love of color and jewelry. I no longer need her acceptance. I found the person who I needed it from all along and that is me! Rest in peace, Mom!

I hope you enjoy this story. It's all true. Every word. Some names have been changed to protect their privacy. All the places and oddball situations are based on actual places and events. Like I have told many people, if I hadn't lived it, I wouldn't believe it!

It was a weird two weeks!

Big love to you all,

Zia

Prologue

"In a memoir, your main contract with the reader is to tell the truth, no matter how bizarre." - Edmund White

If you would have told me three months ago that I would be changing my name, I would have laughed out loud! I finally felt comfortable in my name and had no intention of changing it. But, here I am preparing the court documents to have my name legally changed from Cindy Eubanks to Zia Poe. Really, Zia Poe!

Never have I considered changing my first name. It never crossed my mind. Cindy was who I was; that was my name. I was good with that. However, my last name was a different thing altogether. Being married twice, I had gone through the name change process and struggled with it because of my daughter. She was a young girl when I divorced, and I wanted us to have the same last name. It seemed like something I could do to help her feel stable during a very turbulent and confusing time. So, I kept my first husband's name. In time, I met husband number two and didn't know what to do. After much anguish and consideration, I decided to use my original birth name. That made the most sense. It was, after all, the name I was born with, the name on my birth certificate - Cindy Eubanks. A perfectly good name. As far as I was concerned, I could be her for the rest of my life without regard to marital status or anything else, for that matter.

Well, that's what I thought.

New Mexico

The name "Zia Poe" was whispered to me while driving through the isolated desert near Abiquiu, New Mexico. It felt like a warm whoosh of air blowing through the car. The wind passed, but the name hung in the air. Zia. Zia Poe. It shocked me at first. I had never heard that name or those words together before in my life. Nor had I ever experienced anything remotely like what had just happened - ever! Just hearing those two words together sent chills through my body. There was a power that hit me, and I had a tingling sensation from the top of my head to the tips of my toes. The name felt like it was spoken to me by someone. But, I was driving alone. I grabbed a pen and pad and wrote it down, thinking I would forget (not possible). But it seemed like a sensible thing to do in this wildly insensible situation. Zia Poe . . . Zia Poe. . . where had it come from? Am I going crazy?

The first time I drove over the state line into New Mexico, I felt something. It was distinct and powerful. It felt like a calling to my soul. It's hard to explain, but it was real. I had never felt like that before about land, mountains, a state, but now I did. My first visit was in the late 1980's, and that feeling filled me every time I'd been there since. It's a stirring. A deep, rich, soul calling that I have always held in my heart, and could never shake. I had some affinity with this land. It's called "The Land of Enchantment," so I know I'm not the only one who felt it. Somewhere deep inside me, at a level I didn't completely understand, was something significant for me in New Mexico.

For many years I thought that I would someday end up living there. Over time I have considered moving, even going as far as doing internet searches for homes for sale in different areas of the state. We've taken vacations there and explored areas near Albuquerque and Santa Fe. Part of me believed I had to go, and another part thought it was some kind of fantasy. But one way or another, I knew in my heart New Mexico was calling me. It was just a matter of time.

An Intuitive Painting Retreat

Over 10 years ago, I learned about a process called Painting from the Wild Heart. It's an intuitive painting process developed by Chris Zydel. Once a year she holds a weeklong retreat at the Ghost Ranch Retreat Center in Abiquiu, New Mexico. This is the place where the famous artist Georgia O'Keeffe lived, painted, and spent her final years. Somehow, I had gotten a flyer about it and looked it up online. It seemed the perfect match for me; I loved New Mexico and I loved to create! Creativity was my thing, and I dabbled in most every art form and medium that inspired me. Plus I have always been a process artist, working through personal issues with art. I knew I had to go. It was meant to be; it was a perfect match. However, after looking at the price and location, I just took the flyer and pinned it to the corkboard near my desk. I deemed it impossible, too far (I lived in Ohio), it would cost too much money (we were always living paycheck to paycheck), not enough time (I used my vacation hours for family trips), etc., etc., etc. But, I could dream . . . one day I would go.

About once a year, I cleaned off my board and would find the Painting from Your Wild Heart flyer buried under other flyers, schedules, notes, and cut out magazine articles I was hoping to find time to read. I'd look at it again, dream about going, think about how I could make it happen, then eventually re-pin it to the cleaned board, always thinking to myself, "I'll go next year." That cycle repeated until 2010. We were moving across the country to California, and I was doing some major de-junking and that corkboard with all its pined treasures was unceremoniously thrown into the trash. A fresh start.

In 2012, I joined a mastermind/book study group. As part of this group, we set goals and shared our dreams. The philosophy of the group was to open ourselves to the idea of possibilities. We were learning to think bigger and believe in our dreams. One week we talked about regrets and I told them my story of the Ghost Ranch Retreat and how I could just never make it happen.

One person asked me, "Why don't you go now?"

The question took me by surprise and I really didn't have a good answer. They encouraged me to pursue it, to make it happen! But some part of me had resigned myself to it being some unfulfilled dream. The group wouldn't let me slide and pushed me to look into it. After one of the meetings I decided to do a Google search to see if it still even existed. Sure enough, within a few clicks of the keyboard I found it. The 14th Annual Painting from the Wild Heart Retreat was being held at the Ghost Ranch in New Mexico in just a few short months. It seemed a bit surreal.

I started thinking to myself, "Could this actually happen? Could I finally go after all these years?"

I realized the only thing stopping me was, well, ME! This time I knew I would find a way to go. I wasn't going to stop myself with excuses. The very next week I sent in a deposit and began planning my trip. I even sent a note along with my check thanking Chris Zydel for waiting for me. After 10 years of wishing and longing (and nearly giving up) I was actually signed up and going! This was an interesting turn of events.

What I didn't know at the time, but realize now, is I was planning a trip with destiny. The calling from New Mexico and the workshop I'd being waiting 10 years to attend were going to collide, and my life would never be the same.

Yet, there was still one more component...

A Peacock

Peacocks are beautiful and amazing birds, but I have never given them too much thought. I've seen a few. Once on a road trip to Seattle, we stopped at a farmer's market where 10 or 12 peacocks roamed around freely in an enormous pen. We watched them for a while and took pictures. It was fascinating. The way they opened up their big fan-like tails and showed all their brilliant colored feathers, doing that shaking thing they do, was wild to watch. Other than that, peacocks had never really crossed my radar. Until...

At the first night of the Painting from the Wild Heart Retreat, Chris passed a bag around the circle of women and asked each of us to pick an object out of the bag. We were told not to look at it, just to hold it in our closed hand. One by one we went around the circle and each woman introduced themselves and shared why they had come. Afterwards they opened their hand and discovered what they had chosen. When my turn came I felt around inside the bag; all the objects were small and felt cold and smooth. I had no idea what they could be. I found one that felt right, pulled it out, passed the bag to the next person, and held the object in my closed fist.

"Hi, my name is Cindy Eubanks and I have been wanting to come to this retreat for over 10 years."

I shared some of my story, my reasons for coming and how they had changed over time. I talked about how grateful I was to be here, and how much I was looking forward to the adventure over the next week. Then, I opened my hand, and there was a shiny metal medallion, and rising up from the surface was an embossed image of a beautiful peacock. I was a bit taken aback. Why in the world had I picked a peacock? I was confused and wasn't sure what it had to do with me. I turned it over and on the back, it was engraved with the words "Protection surrounds you during this time of resurrection and rebirth." Umm, that seemed odd.

I thought to myself, "It's just a simple exercise; don't make too much of it."

Most of the other women chose objects that fit them perfectly, and seemed to be very significant. Real synchronicities. I was not sure at all what to make of my peacock. It really didn't resonate with me, but I was willing to keep an open mind. I slipped it into my pocket.

Little did I know what that peacock would represent for me by the end of the week. I didn't see the magic coming . . . but it had arrived.

This is the tale of that magic. How New Mexico, an intuitive painting retreat, and a peacock came to transform my life and open me to a deeper understanding of life, love, and self-acceptance. I am compelled to tell this story. In writing it, I get the opportunity to remember every detail and more fully embrace the experience. But, most importantly, by telling this story I can share what I learned. It's about truth, acceptance, and what it means to be authentic. It's about connecting to the ONENESS we all share. It's a beautiful thing!

Here's my story of Becoming Zia . . .

THE TUMOR NEWS

"Every problem is a gift - without problems we would not grow." - Anthony Robbins

It seemed like I had been waiting forever. Finally, the doctor came into the room.

"Well, I have some good news and some bad news," he said in that doctorly way. "The bad news is you have parathyroid adenoma. That means you have a tumor on your parathyroid gland."

I looked at him, knowing this was going to be the diagnosis, actually feeling sort of relieved. This would explain all the problems I was having, all the weird symptoms. But, I was freaked out too. Thinking it and now having it confirmed were two different things.

"It looks like it's been growing for a number of years, I would estimate five to eight; it seems large in the scan. However, it's hard to tell until we get in there," he explained.

"Surgery?" I said meekly, unintentionally.

"Yes, and the sooner the better."

He wrote some notes in my file.

"Now, the good news. These tumors are most always benign, 99% of the time. Once removed the symptoms begin to subside immediately, and the parathyroid starts functioning normally again."

He then went into detail about the surgery, the recovery, and the aftercare.

"I'll send in the nurse who will schedule your pre-op and the surgery. Do you have any questions?"

I stared at him for a moment.

"No, I think I understand everything," I said.

With that, he left the room.

When I finally left the hospital, it seemed like I was in a movie; the background shot was fuzzy, people were busily walking by, and I was lost in my thoughts. But, it was real life. In a few weeks I was going to have my throat cut open, a tumor removed and . . . Oh yes, the doctor said something about the risk of damaging the vocal cords? What was that he said . . . I was trying to remember. Something about the statistic that one in 250 people have permanent damage, was that right? Oh geez, what if I lost my voice? Oh my God. No way. I started to imagine not having a voice, and it really started to freak me out. Then I started thinking about cancer. There was a 99 percent chance of it being benign. But there is always that possibility . . . my mind was racing.

"Hey lady, watch where you're going!" shouted a man I walked into on the sidewalk.

"Sorry," I said softly.

The encounter brought me back to reality, and I realized I was headed in the wrong direction; my car was on the other side of the building.

* * *

Weeks earlier my naturopath, Dr. Robert Maki, had suspected I may have a tumor on my parathyroid and sent me for tests. My primary physician told me it was rare, and that we would watch the numbers for a few months. Thank goodness I listened to Dr. Maki instead! He had explained the entire issue in detail, so I was prepared for the findings yet really not. Thinking it might be, and actually having it diagnosed is another matter. The bottom line; it was no surprise.

What was surprising is how I reacted to it. The idea of losing my voice, even a remote possibility, hit me hard. Talking was my thing; I loved to talk. I suddenly realized I was also afraid of surgery. Going in the hospital, being put under anesthesia, being cut on, especially my throat, no . . . this is not something I wanted to do.

The next logical question came into my mind, "why? Why am I having another throat issue?"

I'd been struggling with a Hashimoto's Disease, a thyroid disorder, for over 20 years. For the past six years my thyroid had been out of whack, never operating normally. Luckily I found Dr. Maki, who was working closely with me to get it regulated. However, the thyroid is a slow- reacting gland and it seems to take forever to get it balanced. I was feeling frustrated and impatient! Then this, a new issue. The endocrine doctor told me that the thyroid and the parathyroid have entirely separate and completely different functions. So, how can this be? Why am I having this issue too?

For the next few days I carried on with life as usual, but in the back of my mind I kept thinking about my throat. Why was I having two major issues in my throat?

Suddenly, I thought, "throat chakra."

Why hadn't I thought of that sooner? Something was going on with my throat chakra, and I needed to pay attention!

Awakening to the 5th Chakra

Receiving the diagnosis of a tumor on my parathyroid started me thinking beyond the physical. What is going on in my life that was creating these issues in my throat? The first thing I did was get out Louise L. Hay's book "You Can Heal Your Life." Her book is the go-to book for discovering what mental patterns create physical dis-ease in the body. There is a great section in the back that lists almost every body part, disease, or condition you can think of. It is formatted in three parts - Problem, Probable Cause, and New Thought Pattern. I quickly looked up "throat." Here's what I found.

- Throat: Avenue of expression. Channel of creativity.
- Problem: The inability to speak up for one's self. Swallowed anger. Stifled creativity. Refusal to change.
- New Thought Pattern: It's okay to make noise. I express myself freely and joyously. I speak up for myself with ease. I express my creativity. I am willing to change.

Oh boy. When I read that, I knew it was time to face some issues. There was much more going on in my throat than thyroid and parathyroid problems. These problems were the result of something bigger. And I was beginning to realize what that something bigger might be. There was a part of me that knew this internally, as soon as I read it, and another part that was in denial. For most of my life, I have been unable to stand up for myself or even speak up. I am a people pleaser. I'd been living in victim mode for a major part of my life. I knew that I had learned to swallow my anger from a very early age and used food to keep it down. Although I was a very creative person, I could only take my creativity to a certain level and then I would self-sabotage. For years I have been in therapy, support groups, reading self-help books, and following a spiritual journey. With all this work, I was still not able to make lasting changes in my life that felt satisfying. Nor was I ever willing to really change the things I knew in my heart I needed to change. All the knowledge was in my head, but I couldn't put it into action in my life. There was a blockage from the intellect to the heart space. Now I understood. My throat was at the center of all this, and it had been my entire life.

It took a few days to let this sink in. I journaled every day. Slowly I began to recognize all the ways my throat was blocked. How many times I had said "yes" when I really wanted to say "no." Times I was silent when I wanted to speak up for myself. Other times when I told stories and embellished them in hopes people thought I was funny. I wanted them to accept me, all the while there was a tightening and a jitteriness in my throat and esophagus that made it difficult to talk. I remember that feeling distinctly. I thought about all the times I had used food to stuff feelings of anger, shame, and sadness. My throat was the battleground of a lifetime of issues. No wonder I was having these problems.

Over the years I had collected a variety of books on the chakra system, and I dug them all out. I started reading. The more I read, the more awakened I felt. There was no more being in denial for me. It was time to face a lifetime of behaviors and habits that were creating illness in my body. I got the message loud and clear. In my journal, I compiled a list:

- Throat chakra is the passageway/connection between the lower physical chakras and the upper higher self/spiritual chakras.
- Blockage here makes it hard to allow knowledge to fully process - head to heart journey and vice versa.
- Throat allows energies to move through, either inwards or outwards.
- 5th chakra organs are the thyroid and parathyroid. (!)
- Energetic center for self-knowledge, truth, attitudes, hearing, taste, and smell.
- Imbalances may manifest as mental or emotional issues such as difficulty with personal expression, creativity, addiction, criticism, and decision making.
- Inability to speak your own truth.
- Finding yourself saying yes when you want to say no.
- Communication issues.
- Childhood traumas teach to mask feelings, suppressing them and staying stuck, difficulty taking charge of life.
- Difficulty or inability to express anger.
- The throat chakra is like a mouthpiece for the other chakras; if the throat is unbalanced, the others are unbalanced.

According to David Pond, author of "Chakras for Beginners:"

"The opening of the 5th chakra can be a very tumultuous path, because first you have to discover your personal truths, and them express them honestly. This requires a great deal of focus and requires us to challenge our beliefs about who we really are in order to ensure that we are not simply expressing a made-up version of ourselves. When we've explored and discovered our personal truth, we than have to have the courage to express our uniqueness, which can sometimes cause resistance from those around us who prefer that we all follow the societal norms."

After contemplating and reading this information over a few times, I knew I had heard the truth. This was me in a nutshell. My entire life I had learned to stuff my feelings, be a keen observer of others, and work to ignore my own true feelings. Even when I was in therapy and attempting to work through issues, I wasn't entirely honest with myself. There was part of me that was afraid to look too deep, to really speak my truth, because I was so unsure. I was afraid of not being heard, and afraid of being heard and then having to do something about it. Saying "yes" to people was an auto response. It wasn't until later, when complaining to someone else, that I realized I really didn't want to do it at all. Although I had brainwashed myself that if I said yes, the other person would like me or think higher of me. I was looking for love and getting more resentful each day. It was at the point that I was in complete denial of many of my own needs. I was betraying myself, and it was showing up as illness in my throat.

Since 1993, when I witnessed the passing of both of my in-laws, I'd been on a spiritual journey. It was at their bedsides that I experienced something profound that opened my mind and heart to something greater than us (humans). What I witnessed in their transition will never leave me because I came to believe in a deep peace and all-encompassing love, the kind that cannot be put into words. Many people call that force God, but I saw it and felt it as a field of energy that had no beginning or end. No sign that it had arrived, just an energy that swelled like a wave and slowly dissolved, leaving me touched at a soul level. It was a gift I never imagined I'd receive. From that day forward, I have been seeking answers and a better understanding of the force. I have come a long way since 1993, and feel that I have a pretty strong belief system in place. I have found peace with my seeking and have moved into acceptance and surrender. With that came, so I thought, was a clear picture of myself and my place in life. However, when I got this diagnosis of a tumor, I realized there was a big part of me that was yet to be healed. There was a teaching in this, a lesson for me, and an awakening to come. I had long known that things like this are not random; they happen for a reason. My throat had a message for me. I had no idea where to start, but I knew I had to find a way to heal myself.

Posting a message on Facebook seemed like a good idea. "Hey, yoga friends. I am in need of some 5th chakra healing. Any ideas?"

Since I used to belong to a loving yoga community in Ohio, I was sure someone could give me a suggestion or two. Meanwhile, I started to pay attention to speaking my own truth and what that really meant to me. Louise Hay had some suggestions on affirmations for the throat, so I posted them on my bathroom mirror.

I am willing to change!

I am willing to face my fears!

I am willing to release all resistance!

(Ask my thyroid and parathyroid) How can I love you back to health?

Every day I looked in the mirror and stated the affirmations with meaning. Knowing that it was a long shot, but what did I have to lose? I began watching my behavior, and practiced saying "no" to a few people.

Then I took a real risk and wrote a long letter to my ex-sister-in-law telling her my feelings about being married to her brother and what that did to me and our daughter. I was telling her things I had held back for decades, and I was scared to death, but also wanted her to know how I felt. She had been my friend for nearly 40 years and I had never been totally honest with her. As I wrote, tears streamed down my face and I felt a flood of emotions pouring out of my body. After writing it I quickly sent it, before I changed my mind. I was fearful of her reaction, but also knew she loved me, so it felt safer. It was not her reaction or her validation I needed, it was finally speaking my truth, sharing it with someone who I knew would hear me. I didn't need a response. This was big. I knew it signified that things were beginning to change.

Once I started paying attention to my behaviors, thoughts, and habits, I could clearly see that I had a big problem. I had been in denial for a long time. I was living a lie, being a person or a persona that I thought people would like and appreciate. Most of it was ego driven, attempting to get love and acceptance. I was really not sure how to change it. I had lived this way so long that it was deeply entrenched. But, one way or another, I was committed to making the change.

I had signed up for the Painting from the Wild Heart retreat in New Mexico, and it was only a few weeks away. I thought that this would be a great opportunity for me to have some quiet time for self-exploration and gain some insights into my newly discovered 5th chakra issues. I didn't know what to expect, but I was hoping for something meaningful.

Suddenly it occurred to me that I could extend the trip and really make time for some soul searching. A private escape to explore all these issues. Originally, I'd made arrangements to fly into Albuquerque the day before the retreat and fly out the day it ended. But now I thought I could cancel my flight and the rental car and drive myself. It was only 800 miles and I could go early, stay a few extra days, and make it an adventure. The idea excited me. I thought about it for a couple of days, then decided to cancel my plane and car reservations. Next, I got on TripAdvisor and started designing my new plan. By the end of the day, I had hotel reservations in several places and had extended my trip from a week to two weeks. Two weeks in New Mexico, all alone, with plenty of time to explore and contemplate this new awareness. A perfect adventure!

LET THE HEALING BEGIN

"May you hear and speak truth. May your life and your creations express the fullness of who you are. May you know ever deeper levels of truth." - Author Unknown

A few days before I left for New Mexico, I met my friend Kat at Starbucks for coffee and to catch up on our lives. I told her all about my recent diagnosis and my upcoming trip. She told me all about her work and shared her latest adventures.

Suddenly she asked, "Hey, do you want to go across the street to that new junk shop? There are some old vintage cameras I have on hold and I want you to take a look at them."

"Sure," I answered.

Kat was a photographer for a travel company and had just started a collection of vintage cameras. We packed up our stuff and headed across the street.

The shop was new in town, and I had been wanting to check it out. As we walked up the front sidewalk, I knew it was going to be an interesting place. They had old furniture, statues, fountains, and lots of repurposed vintage items everywhere. There was even a small garden. We walked in, and a little bell rang over the door. Behind the counter was a woman and she welcomed us to the store. As soon as I looked at her I knew I had met her before, but I couldn't remember when, where, or how.

She looked at me with the same quizzical look and I said, "I know you from somewhere."

"Yes," she said, "but I am not sure where I know you from?"

"Me either," I replied.

But, slowly something was coming back to me.

"I think I met you at a woman's circle in Phelan."

Another friend, Genia, had introduced us. We all rode together to the circle.

"I think we both know Genia," I said.

"That's right! We all drove together to that gathering. Oh yes, that's it! I'm Tamara."

"Yes, I remember now! I'm Cindy. So, you work here. That must be fun."

"Actually, I have a space here. And I work the counter occasionally."

"Space? What kind of space?" I asked.

Somehow, I thought she was connected to Genia through the real estate industry. Genia was a real estate agent.

"I do chakra balancing and Reiki," Tamara said.

I nearly laughed out loud. Just a few days ago I put out into the universe that I needed some 5th chakra healing. Sure, I put it out into the world via Facebook, but apparently the message traveled in other realms too.

"Wow, this is a coincidence. I am looking for some help balancing my chakras," I said with a little surprise.

I then told her about my parathyroid tumor and my realization of the throat chakra issues.

"Well, come on back and let me show you my space. And, I'll explain what I do."

I followed her through the maze of antiques and collectables, shabby chic furniture, and handcrafted works of art. Towards the back of the store was a little room. Some of the walls were made out of beautiful stained glass. In the center was a massage table and surrounding it was a collection of bookcases covered with gemstones, figures, cards of all types, sage, candles, and a platform that had a mediation area and a giant crystal singing bowl.

I slowly took it all in as she began to explain to me about Reiki and how she does her charka alignments. I have known about Reiki for years and have some friends who are practitioners, but I had never had a session. There was something about her and this space that mesmerized me, and I knew I had to make an appointment with her. I was leaving for New Mexico in just a couple of days, and I really wanted to do this before I left. I knew this was not just a chance meeting; this was part of a bigger plan. How big I could never have imagined at that point, but it was the beginning.

She agreed to see me that Monday at 7 pm. It was Labor Day, but she was very accommodating. She knew I really wanted to do this. I was leaving on my adventure early Tuesday morning, and I couldn't think of a better way to start off my journey.

Just before I left she handed me a bottle of water and said, "Drink this between now and when I see you. When it gets empty, fill it with filtered water."

I looked at the bottle, which said Starfire Water Sacred Sound Resonance Transmission.

"You may think it's weird, but just do it," she added.

I nodded my head yes.

"Have your ever heard of Dr. Masaru Emoto?" she asked me.

Oddly enough I had. He was the Japanese researcher who had done experiments with ice crystals using different music, sounds, and words. His work was extraordinary. He examined ice crystals after they had been exposed to a variety of different music, from rock-n-roll to classical. Each crystal created a different formation when exposed to the music - the more beautiful the music, the more beautiful the crystals. He then put water in jars marked with different words and did the same experiment with the same results. Words like love and peace created beautiful crystals, and words like hate and war created scattered and misshapen crystals.

"Yes," I told her, "I've seen pictures of his work and read about him. Very interesting stuff."

"Think of this water in that way. It is water that has cosmic healing energy. Even after you drink the water, refill the bottle and it will be infused with the same energy. I just got this, and you are the first person I am giving some to."

I thanked Tamara and walked out into the store to find Kat and check out the vintage cameras. Was I ever happy that I met her for coffee that day. Serendipitous!

* * *

Over the next two days, I gathered everything I thought I would need for my trip and packed my car. By 5 pm on Labor Day I was ready. Everything was stowed. I had downloaded a few books on tape from Overdrive to my iPad, and all my electronic gear was in the front seat. I had food, water, paints, an easel, my favorite comforter, pillows, and an oscillating fan. Everything I needed, and more. I was prepared for my journey.

Just after 6:30 pm, I headed off to meet Tamara for my chakra balancing appointment. The sun was setting and it was a warm, still evening. It was one of those beautiful days in the desert where the sunset just takes your breath away. I was feeling excited, a little apprehensive, and filled with anticipation to begin my journey the next day. This Reiki session would be the perfect start for the trip. I felt like an ancient adventurer having a ceremonial ritual for my impending spiritual quest.

Tamara was waiting for me when I arrived. The shop was closed and we were all alone. It was quiet, peaceful, and inviting. She had some beautiful music playing gently in the background, the lights were low, and candles were burning. We sat down together, and she pulled out several sets of divination cards.

"Look these over and pick one that feels right for you," she instructed.

There were Angel cards, Symbol cards, Animal Totem cards, Goddess cards, and Ascended Master cards. I was immediately drawn to the Ascended Master deck. I picked it up.

"Okay, open them, shuffle the cards, and then choose one when you are ready," she instructed.

I did as she said. I held the cards in my hands. When it felt right, I pulled one from the deck and handed it to her.

"Ah. You have chosen Thoth. Do you write?" she asked.

I laughed.

"Yes, as a matter of fact I have been working on a book since 2007. I'm actually kind of stuck and I put it on hold in July. But I am still writing; I keep a daily journal on my laptop."

That wasn't completely the truth. I had been on schedule to complete and publish my book in June, and couldn't do it. I felt like a fraud, a phony. The subject of my book was body image and weight loss, and I was still struggling with my own issues around this topic more than ever. How could I publish this book when I had so much to figure out myself? This was a hot-button issue for me. I felt a rush of shame and regret flow through me, but I quickly let it go.

"You need to keep writing," she encouraged. "When you draw Thoth, it is all about writing. And this has some high energy for you."

She handed me the card.

It looked sort of Egyptian and showed an image of Thoth and it read:

You drew this card as a concrete reminder to write. You've been receiving lots of signs and feeling to write lately, so let this card be the message that leads you to take action. Don't worry about punctuation, grammar, or spelling, as you can take care of that later. Your life's purpose involves writing. Write an article or book.

As I held this card in my hand and read these words, I knew it was true. This was off to an interesting start. I wasn't sure what to think. Of all the multitude of cards in this deck, I pick the one that has to do with writing. Writing had been my main focus for months. Before I learned about my parathyroid tumor, the issue I wanted to address during my retreat to New Mexico was my self-sabotage around my writing. For months, I had been diligently working on completing my book. I even developed a website, a workbook, and a workshop that would help teach the principles. I had a cover designer, a book editor, and had begun advertising for a test group for my workshop format. But I couldn't finish. I was stuck. Something was stopping me; it just didn't feel right. I was so frustrated and confused! Now, I get this card.

Tamara must have sensed my energy shift.

"Well, let's get started. Take off your shoes, get up on the table, and make yourself comfortable. Keep your hands at your sides."

I used the small step she had by the table to lift myself up on the table and then laid down. She slid a pillow under my knees, covered me with a light blanket, and asked if I was comfortable.

"Yes," I answered with a big sigh.

"Do you know how to do yoga breathing?"

I nodded.

"Great. I am going to play a breathing mediation and all you have to do is follow along. Just breathe and relax. During the session, I'll be placing crystals on your body and I may burn some sage, so don't be surprised when that happens."

I had already started some slow, deep breathing and was beginning to relax into the soft, warm, comfortable table. The music started and it was beautiful, slow, and soothing. A woman's voice gently started speaking, guiding me into a deep, slow breathing sequence. Within a few minutes I was totally relaxed and at ease. I began to feel like I had been transported to another place. I had no concept of being in the room at all.

Then I began to notice the heat of Tamara's hands above my feet. I knew her hands were there, but I didn't feel her touching me. All I felt was a warm sensation. She moved very slowly from my feet, then up my legs and on to my mid-section. There was a gentle sensation when she placed crystals on my body, but I barely noticed. The breathing meditation woman had stopped speaking, but I was still taking long, slow, deep breaths. Gentle, esoteric music floated around the room. It felt like an altered state. Her hands were radiating so much heat it felt like I was being warmed by a fire. She covered every area of my body. The process was so gentle, nearly in slow motion. When she got to my head she spent a lot of time on my scalp, ears, neck, and then my throat. She cupped her hands near my throat, and I felt the energy like a bolt of lightning. It was energizing, yet very soothing. Slowly I began to relax into it and go even more deeply into the experience.

Then suddenly, yet very gently, I began to separate from the physical experience altogether. I became aware of an image, a woman's face just above my third eye area. My entire focus now shifted towards this image. My eyes were closed tight, but I could see the image in my mind's eye. It felt so real, and it was becoming more and more clear, but there was still a hazy, sort of foggy effect around the edges. Had I not been in this situation and a somewhat altered state I would have been alarmed. But it felt as natural as anything I had ever experienced. The face began to get clearer and come into focus and I could see it was my mother's face, but she looked like an angel. There was a softness and sweetness about her. She was beautiful. I had a total sensation of my heart opening to her beauty, the amazing soft, gentle, loving sweetness of her beauty. Tears began to leak from my eyes, and my entire body felt warm with a pure overwhelming sense of love. There was an odd feeling that arose. I sensed that I was holding on to her and she wanted to be released. She looked at such peace with a sweet softness to her smile; she was telling me she wanted to go, and that it was okay. But she wasn't saying a word. The feelings of it just pulsed through my body. This sense was like a knowing; I knew in my heart and head that it was time for me to let her go. It was time for me to be a full-grown adult, to become the woman I am, and step into my true essence. I knew it was time to let go of pleasing her, or wanting her approval, or blaming her for my issues, and just remember her as this beautiful angel. Whether it was a physical letting go or a metaphysical letting go, it was real and profound. Her beauty was still radiating right above my head, and she began to slowly disappear. As she began to vanish, I was aware that Tamara had begun playing the crystal bowl and I could smell sage burning.

The sound was coming from behind me, and it was getting louder and louder. It was clear and harmonic and felt like it was filling the room with the vibration. I could begin to feel the vibrations through my entire body. Then I suddenly felt it deep in my throat - it was making my throat quiver, and the energy radiated out through my entire body. Without even thinking, out of some primal instinct, I began to hum along with the sound. The moment I started to hum, the vibrating in my throat intensified and the sound began to resonate out from my throat chakra. It got louder and louder, and I hummed more and more and the feeling grew and grew. My mind imagined that my tumor was being swallowed up in the energy force being created and would just disappear. It felt like nothing I had ever felt before. Then, it even got louder. Tamara was playing the bowl with such energy and power the sound was bouncing off the walls and through my body. I felt like I was being lifted off the table.

The sound had reached a crescendo, and she let it continue to vibrate and slowly soften. I connected with my breathing and just allowed myself to feel the amazing experience. It seemed like forever as the bowl softened, getting more and more quiet until it eventually faded into silence. The room was completely still - you could have heard a pin drop. I lay there, allowing myself to absorb what had just happened.

"Cindy, it's time to come back into the room now. Gently wiggle your fingers and toes," Tamara said quietly near my ear.

My eyes had been closed tightly and the room seemed very dark when I opened them. I did as she asked and also stretched my arms and legs. I lay there for a few minutes and then sat up. It felt like I had been transported from another world. I looked at the clock and nearly an hour and half had passed. That seemed impossible.

"So, how was that?" she asked me.

"Hard to describe, but wonderful!" I sighed. "That bowl was something else!"

"Yes," she exclaimed. "I've never played it that long or that loud before. Wasn't it really loud?"

"Yes!" I said. "It felt like it was vibrating the whole room!"

"I know. Something just kept telling me to play it, so I did!"

"Well, I am glad you did. I feel like my throat may be healed. Isn't that crazy!"

We both laughed. Partly because it was such a unique experience and partly because both of us thought it could very well be true!

On the table beside her was a layout of stones and crystals. She had laid them out in the same order she had placed them on my body. I was shocked. There were at least a dozen or more stones. Some of them were rather large, and I had no idea they had been resting on me. I had only felt one or two. She explained to me what they all meant and the areas of my body that were weak or strong. It was beautiful to look at, and I could feel the energy radiating from the stones. She told she would leave them laid out overnight to hold energy for me as I began my journey to New Mexico.

It felt like I had just received a precious gift. Never in my life had I had an experience like that. My head was filled with questions, but I also felt like I understood. All I needed was some time to process. I thanked her profusely, and she walked me to my car. It was so dark outside and suddenly seemed so isolated. I was grateful she did. During the session, the wind had started to blow and it was blowing hard. The sky was crystal clear, and the stars were shining brightly. With the dark, midnight blue sky, the strong, hot wind, and the twinkling of the stars I felt like magic was in the air. My body was still tingling, and I knew something unique and mystical had just happened. Not sure what to make of it, I started the car and drove towards home. My journey had begun.

LESSONS ON THE ROAD

"A good traveler has no fixed plans, and is not intent on arriving." - Lao Tzu

It was a fitful night's sleep. The excitement about the trip and the chakra healing with Tamara had me a bit off kilter. Plus, knowing the alarm was going off at 4 am didn't help. But I was awake and the day had arrived - I was going to New Mexico. I was up before the alarm, showered, dressed, and out the door before 4:30 am. It was still pitch dark outside. It had an eerie feeling in the pre-dawn hours. The rest of the world was asleep, and this was the time before life started. Part of me was excited; part of me was a bit anxious. Taking off in the seeming dead of night and driving out to the middle of the desert, alone, seemed a little daunting. On the other hand, taking off by myself for a two-week adventure in New Mexico was exhilarating. I was little bit scared, but a lot excited!

When I entered the ramp onto Interstate 15, everything changed - it seemed the world had come alive. The freeway was filled with travelers and truckers, headlights shining in both directions. I was headed east, and had made up my mind that I would make it to Needles, California for breakfast. The sun would start its rise in a couple of hours and I loved that feeling. It made the trip more special. Waking up early, heading out in the dark, and then watching the dawn of a new day over the horizon. It was awe inspiring, especially in the wide-open desert; it seemed like a spiritual experience! When I was a kid, my parents always planned our trips this way. It was that memory along with the anticipation of this adventure that had me feeling warm, happy, and excited!

Before long the excitement I had started with turned into a bit of boredom as the desert and the road stretched out dry, flat, and straight in front of me. I had over 100 miles before I reached Needles, so I decided to listen to an audio book. I reviewed the list on my iPad and selected Geneen Roth's latest book, "Lost and Found: One Woman's Story of Losing Her Money and Finding her Life." It was the story of losing all her savings in the Bernie Madoff debacle and how she came to a new understanding of money. But more than that, it was about behaviors with money and food and how the two were intertwined. Roth is an author of several books about relationships with food, and she also promotes giving up dieting. I had been reading her books since the 1980's. It seemed she might have an interesting twist on money. Since food, weight, and dieting were big issues in my life, along with money, budgeting, and shopping, I thought it might give me some insight.

Sure enough, I picked the right book. As she spoke, my mind connected her stories with my life and all kinds of crazy behaviors. There were so many similarities. While I listened, a sentence or two would jump out at me and my mind would grab hold of the thought and get lost. On several occasions, I had to rewind back to where I had drifted off. There were a few things she talked about that had hit a strong chord, and I knew I wanted to delve into deeper. It was one of those moments when it felt extremely clear that there was some big learning for me.

I got off at the next off ramp, grabbed a notebook and pen, and wrote down the following sentences that had hit me when I heard her speak them.

- You can't be shamed into consciousness.
- Rebellion is the other side of compliance, but it is not freedom.
- If you think being thin makes you happy, then all thin people would be happy. If you think having lots of money makes you happy, then everyone with lots of money would be happy.
- Stop living to protect yourself from losses that have already happened.

Once I was back on the road, I turned off the audio. I thought about each of the four sentences, each one an opening for insights into my own healing. Her words profound. Ideas I never contemplated before but as soon as I heard them, rang within me as a long-forgotten truth.

Here are some of my "a-ha" moments from the road.

"You can't be shamed into consciousness."

> Biggie! For nearly five years I have been living with shame, hoping it would enlighten me. Back in 2001, I lost over 170 pounds and kept it off for years. An amazing success! I felt fabulous and thought I really had the weight problem licked. Never would I have to deal with this problem again. I would live the rest of my life thin and happy. As a matter of fact, the book I was writing (and shelved) was about this transition and what I learned from it. The book is called "Body

Belief: A New Paradigm in Weight Loss and Body Image." However, in 2009 I started gaining weight and before the year's end, I had gained back nearly eighty pounds. I felt so self-conscious and ashamed; I couldn't believe this was happening to me. Since then I have been trying to lose what I had gained with no success. In the meantime I am writing this book, and feel like a total failure and fraud. All while I have been using shame to motivate me and attempt to snap me into action, and take off this weight again. When I heard these words, "you can't be shamed into consciousness," I felt a huge shift. How could I be successful at anything if I used shame as the motivator?

"Rebellion is the other side of compliance, but it's not freedom."

Oh, this was about polarity - opposites. When I heard this, I had a flashback. For years I followed a yoga master, Amrit Desai. He talked constantly about duality and how it was the cause of suffering. Choosing one side or the other draws your focus and attention, either for or against.

He always said, "Where attention goes, energy follows."

As soon as you said, "I like it!" or "I don't like it!" you are choosing to suffer.

What Geneen said hit the nail on the head. Rebellion is the opposite of compliance, being attached to either of them will create struggle and pain, and there will never be freedom in your life. At that moment I realized I had been swinging from compliance to rebellion my entire life, looking for freedom. I did it with money, and I did it with food. Never having peace or success with either. This was a life-shifting realization!

"If you think being thin makes you happy, then all thin people would be happy. If you think having lots of money makes you happy, then everyone with lots of money would be happy."

This is all or nothing thinking. Deep down inside of me I equate happiness with being thin. When I lie in bed at night, the two main topics of the mental chatter that keep me awake are thoughts about losing weight and concerns about money. Constant obsessing about being fat and figuring out how to get thin and/or worrying about money, not having enough, and how to get more. So it makes sense that if these things were fixed, I would be happy. Or at least happier. On an intellectual level, I totally get that this is not true, but in some kind of "if a magic genie showed up" kind of way I believe it. This made me realize I need to figure how to be happy despite the things that get me down. What would it be like to accept myself exactly at the weight I am today? Get up in the morning, get dressed, and get on with my day. Or be content with the fact that I have enough money to live comfortably and do many things other people see as luxuries. Like getting up each day and doing exactly what I want to do. That's huge! Happiness isn't a dress size or a number in your bank account. I get that, but it's hard for me. Especially the weight issue. Having been fat and having been thin, I can tell you thin is much better. I felt healthier, happier, and my life opened up in ways I never imagined. It's figuring out that these things aren't necessary for happiness that I've got to understand.

"Stop living to protect yourself from loses that have already happened."

No matter how many art supplies I buy or chocolate peanut clusters I eat, I can never go back and protect myself from being molested, or living in a dysfunctional home isolated in the Mojave Desert, or having a father with severe PTSD and a narcissistic Mom with a "nervous" disorder. It happened; it was my life. It is in the past, and there is no way spending money or binge eating is going to fix that. When I heard her words, it was like a big neon sign was lit in the road in front of me. How could a few short words make so much sense and I had never, ever thought of it? Well, maybe I had heard it said but not the way I heard it that day driving in my car in the middle of nowhere. It hit me like a ton of bricks. I had been living my life trying to protect myself from pain that was long over, gone, history. Using money and food to soothe decades-old losses. When was I willing to let that go and move into today?

After several miles and a lot of reflection I realized that I was holding on to these stories, those past events, like a badge of honor. I used them as an excuse for all the failures in my life and as a weapon to beat myself up. The losses were my pillars, part of my foundation. How could I let them go? I knew that it was unlikely, well, actually impossible to be hurt the way I had been then. I was older, so much wiser, and could never be that innocent and naive. But I knew, deep in my heart, that I had to stop living to protect myself from those losses. It made perfect sense. But I also had to stop identifying with them, using them as part of my foundation and armor. Who would I be if I stopped hanging on to those losses? Good question.

The sun had risen, I had stopped and eaten breakfast in Needles, and I was well on my way to Gallup, New Mexico. After breakfast, I returned to the audio book, ready to get more insights. My head was already spinning with thoughts and revelations about my life. It was my first day of the journey and I was already deep into it. The solitude of the road and Geneen's words began to open me in a way I had never expected. It was about truth and really being honest with myself. Seeing myself in a new light and being open to whatever came forth. It felt good.

*   *   *

By early afternoon, I was in Gallup. I decided to spend the rest of the afternoon exploring old Route 66. I had just started down the road when I saw a sign for the Navajo Thunderbird Jewelry Supply Store, and decided to check it out. It looked intriguing, so I pulled into the parking lot. The inside of the store was filled with stones, findings, wire, silver, and tools. Anything you needed to make almost any type of jewelry, specifically anything Native American with turquoise, coral, and silver. It was like finding a hidden treasure. I looked at every display case and shelf.

After a half hour or so, I looked around and suddenly realized I was the only white person in the store. Many of the Native Americans in the store were watching me. I began to feel uncomfortable. It felt like I was breaking some boundary, like I was trespassing on sacred ground. The discomfort I felt was overpowering, so I went to the checkout, paid for the few things I had picked up, and left the store. It occurred to me that this store was the place Native Americans bought their supplies to make jewelry to sell to people like me. Even knowing that I wasn't the only tourist to have stopped here, I still had a peculiar feeling vibrating within me.

Once in the car, I sat for a moment and thought about what I had just experienced. It was odd, but felt very real to me. Suddenly, I noticed a young Native man walking towards my car. He looked like he could hardly walk, his clothes were dirty, his hair disheveled. I realized as he got closer that he was drunk. He looked at me with dark, pleading eyes and I rolled my window down a few inches. He spoke something to me I couldn't understand, but before he could repeat himself, a security guard appeared from out of nowhere. He said something to the young man, who turned and walked away in a knowing way.

The guard said, "Sorry, ma'am."

My heart was racing a bit; I was feeling vulnerable and a bit shocked. Where had the security guard come from? What had the young man asked me? I watched as he walked past the building and down the street.

The thing about crossing over the state line of New Mexico is the sudden awareness that you are in Indian country. Especially in Gallup. There was something going on with me and this feeling of being an outsider that I was not sure I liked. I was also filled with a feeling of white guilt and a huge heaviness of sorrow. The truth is I had been born with two strong traits that have followed me throughout my life. The first is being extremely empathic. I have the ability to see and feel others' pain, joy, and sorrow, whether it shows on the surface or not. The second truth is I was born a bleeding-heart liberal. Don't know how that happened since I was born into a Republican family, but I am. There was never a time in my life that I can't remember questioning my family's political beliefs when it came to social issues or anything people-related. Being in a city where the population is mostly Native American with poverty apparent in every direction I looked made me innately aware and uncomfortable. Being in that store that serviced local people so they could make jewelry to sell to people like me felt wrong. I was looking for bargains, and I could suddenly see myself through their eyes. Then, having the encounter with the young Native man and the security guard made me want to be anywhere else than in the parking lot of that store.

I got back on Route 66 and drove through town towards my hotel. I'd been here many times before, but this day I was seeing Gallup with different eyes. It has a uniqueness all its own, but there is a sadness factor that seems to be part of the fabric of the city. This city is one of the hubs for the most amazing silver and turquoise jewelry in the country. The creativity and talent here are without comparison. But along with that is something more - sadness, struggle, and a sense of hopelessness. It was a heavy feeling. People living their lives, going through the motions, but knowing their future was more of the same. Dreams seemed like a scarce commodity. I thought of the young man in the parking lot and wondered how many more people struggled with alcoholism and drug addictions. His face left a haunting memory etched into my mind.

Later, I stopped at a restaurant to get some dinner. After I ordered, I glanced around the place and realized that I was again the only white person in the room. It felt strange and I started to wonder why I was choosing to have this experience today. Or who was choosing it for me. When my order arrived I asked the waitress to pack it up to go, and I headed off to the hotel.

Once I checked in and unloaded my things, I ate my dinner and got ready for bed. It had been a long day, getting up before 4 am, listening to the audio book and having some major revelations, and then the experiences I just had, it was time for some sleep. I checked the time on my phone; it was 6:30 pm. It didn't matter; I turned off the lights, snuggled under the covers, and I was out like a light.

Meeting Mr. Gloom in Santa Fe

*"Tell me, has anything odd happened to you recently? What do
you mean, odd? Unusual. Deviating from the customary.
Something outside the usual parameters of normalcy. An
occurrence of unprecedented weird." - Jasper Forde*

I was up early again and on my way to Santa Fe before 5 am,
feeling a bit relieved to be leaving Gallup. It was a beautiful
morning; the sun was coming up and I had less than 300
miles to drive. I had an entirely new attitude and a whole day
ahead of me to explore Santa Fe. This is what I had been
looking forward to for weeks. Time to explore Santa Fe
without thinking of anyone but myself. My own adventure. I
could go where I wanted, see what I wanted, and eat where I
wanted. Quality me time.

In the miles between Gallup and Santa Fe, more than the
scenery changes. As the road turned in a northerly direction
just before Albuquerque, the climb to Santa Fe began. The
closer to Santa Fe, the more affluent it seemed to get. At first
there was just a smattering of houses, mostly modern-day
adobes, then the city grew out of the high chaparral. The feel
there was entirely different than what I had experienced the
day before. Santa Fe had a beauty all its own. It had a feeling
of history but also a lot of creative energy, unique unto itself.

That feeling is what draws visitors here from all over the world, including me.

Once I was close, I entered the address of my hotel into my iPhone's map and found it with ease. The Sage Inn was just about a mile from the old historical Plaza area. It was too early to check in, but I thought I would give it a try. I parked and found my way to the front desk. The desk clerk was busy with a couple checking out. Looking around the lobby, I saw a big sign behind the counter that read "Fiestas de Santa Fe" and on the end of the counter was a strange-looking creature. It was about three feet tall and had what looked like a sheet draped over it, with a big bow tie and cuffs. It had a head with giant ears and big bulgy black and green eyes, big red lips, orange hair, and two skinny arms with huge hands and extremely large index fingers. The index fingers seemed to be pointing. It was kind of creepy. Actually, it was very creepy. The couple finished up, and I walked up to the desk.

"Hi, I have a reservation for tonight and tomorrow night. I know it's early, but I thought I would check to see if you have a room ready," I explained to the woman behind the desk.

"Let me check," she responded with a smile.

She asked my name and looked up my reservation.

"Here it is. Must be your lucky day; the room just finished being cleaned."

As she took all my info and prepared the key cards, I asked, "Who is the creepy guy on the counter?"

"Zozobra?" she looked at me quizzically. "Aren't you here for the Fiesta?"

I shook my head no.

"I'm here for a couple of days to explore before I head to the Ghost Ranch for a retreat."

"How about that. Most everyone is here for the Fiesta. Every place in town gets booked up nearly a year in advance. Thursday night Zozobra gets burned, and then Friday morning the Fiesta begins. You sure picked the right time to come."

"Zozobra gets burned?" I said with a puzzled look.

It was Wednesday morning and I was staying until Friday afternoon. Good timing, I suppose, if I knew what was happening.

"Sure, this is the 89th year!" she said.

She went on to tell a bit of the history of Zozobra and the Fiesta.

"Zozobra is called Old Man Gloom. He represents all the things people want to let go of from the past year; you know all the bad stuff. For the past couple of weeks there have been 50-gallon barrels around town, and you can write down what you want to let go of and drop it in one of them. Some people put things in there. Like one woman I know put her wedding dress in after she got a divorce. Then the city picks it up, and they take it all and stuff it in Zozobra, and then he gets burned up. That signifies the beginning of a new year, and then the Fiesta begins. Everyone is freed from all their problems," she laughed.

"Oh, that sounds interesting and kind of weird. Where do they burn him?" I asked.

"At Fort Mercy Park. He'll be there today; they have to bring him in a big truck and use a crane to set him up."

"A crane?"

"Yep, he's over 50 feet tall."

I was having a hard time getting my mind around what she was saying. A 50-foot-tall "thing" stuffed with the entire city's regrets, worries, problems, and actual "things" they wanted to release. Now that was interesting. I was going to have to learn more about this.

She gave me the key to my room and a map of the old town. She marked on the map where Zozobra would be burned.

"It'll be getting pretty crowded around here soon. There is not much parking downtown, so we provide a shuttle every hour on the hour until 9 pm. Just be out front, and the van will be waiting. You can't miss it," she explained.

I thanked her and went to find my room. It seemed my time in Santa Fe was going to be more interesting than I expected.

My room was great. It had an interesting, old Santa Fe feel. I could park my car right in front of my door, which made unloading all my junk easy. It had a great view of a new park just completed across the street. I unpacked and settled in, got out my laptop, hooked up to the Wi-Fi, and did a Google search for Zozobra. I needed to find out more.

Much to my surprise, Zozobra popped up right away with many, many interesting pictures of him being burned. I clicked on a page to learn more.

> *Each year The Kiwanis Club of Santa Fe stages the burning of Zozobra, kicking off the annual Fiestas de*

Santa Fe. Zozobra centers around the ritual burning in effigy of Old Man Gloom, to dispel the hardships and travails of the past year.

The Fiestas celebration began in 1712 to celebrate an expedition by Don Diego de Vargas, who reconquered the territory of New Mexico. Zozobra became part of the Fiestas in 1926, and the Kiwanis club began sponsoring the burning in 1963 as its major fundraiser. Local artist William Howard Shuster, Jr. (1893-1969) conceived and created Zozobra in 1924 as the focus of a private fiesta at his home for artists and writers in the community. His inspiration for Zozobra came from the Holy Week celebrations of the Yaqui Indians of Mexico; an effigy of Judas, filled with firecrackers, was led around the village on a donkey and later burned. Shuster and E. Dana Johnson, a newspaper editor and friend of Shuster's came up with the name Zozobra, which was defined as "anguish, anxiety, gloom" or in Spanish for "the gloomy one."

The effigy is a giant animated wooden and cloth marionette that waves its arms and growls ominously at the approach of its fate. A major highlight of the pageant is the fire spirit dancer, dressed in a flowing red costume, who appears at the top of the stage to drive away the white-sheeted "glooms" from the base of the giant Zozobra. The fire dance was created by Jacques Cartier, a former New York ballet dancer and local dance teacher, who performed the role for 37 years. His dance student, James Lilienthal took over the fire spirit role in 1970 and has continued it for 32 years.

Shuster constructed the figure of Zozobra until 1964, when he gave his detailed model to the Kiwanis Club to continue the tradition. Over the years the effigy has grown larger, reaching a height of 49 feet. Zozobra is a well-crafted framework of preplanned and pre-cut sticks, covered with chicken wire and yards of muslin. It is stuffed with bushels of shredded paper, which traditionally includes obsolete police reports, paid off mortgage papers, and even personal divorce papers.

After doing the research I felt a little better informed, and I was getting excited about being part this unique experience. It seemed like another synchronistic step in this journey I was on. I needed to figure out a way I could get my "glooms" into Zozobra, so they could get burned up too. So, I jumped in the car and went looking for Fort Mercy Park.

It didn't take long to find it, or, at least to get near it. Unfortunately, the roads were blocked in every direction. It was clear this was a big deal. I found a place to stop near the park, but I couldn't get out. I caught a glimpse of Zozobra before a city worker waved at me to move my car. It was huge! Gigantic. Fifty feet is a lot taller than I imagined. The little Zozobra I saw on the counter of the hotel didn't do justice to the real thing. About a block up the road, I turned around, made another pass, and took a second quick look. Wild! This was going to be one unique experience. I couldn't wait until Thursday night. Meanwhile, I had lots of other sights to see. Off I headed for the Plaza.

Old Town Santa Fe and the Plaza are unique and an integral part of the city. Just one square block with a city park in the center, surrounded by shops and restaurants. Over the years, the shops and eateries have spread from the Plaza center outwards for blocks. There is so much to see it takes days.

The city government of Santa Fe is the longest running city government in the country. This is an old city. And the Plaza is at its heart. The feeling of their history just hangs in the air.

I drove around looking for a parking space. Lots of parking was blocked in preparation for the Fiesta. Everywhere I drove, spots were either tagged or full. After a while I remembered that the hotel had a shuttle and decided to go back, park my car, and take the shuttle back to the Plaza.

The shuttle was parked in front of the hotel when I arrived. I quickly parked my car and walked over to it. A young man was standing by the van door. We were the only two there.

"Are you heading to the Plaza?" he asked.

"Yes. Taking the shuttle seems like the smart thing to do. I was just down there and couldn't find a place to park," I told him.

"Yeah, it'll be like that all weekend. But we're here every hour on the hour if you need a lift. Looks like you're the only one for now. Hop in and let's go."

He held open the front door of the big 12-passenger van for me, and I climbed in.

You could tell he was a local; he had that feeling about him. I imagined he was a young college student, working for the hotel part-time to help pay for college. Or he was a local who dreamed of getting out of Santa Fe and exploring the world, but was stuck working at this hotel to make ends meet until he could escape.

 "Are you from around here?" I asked.

"Yep, born and raised," he answered.

"You like doing this?"

"It's okay. Better than some jobs, worse than others. But I like the freedom. Plus, I get to talk to all the people who come through. People come from all over the world," he said in an interesting, sort of flippant way.

"I was going to college, but I quit," he continued. "I'm not sure what I am going to do, but this pays the bills."

Since he was a local, I thought I could get more information from him about Zozobra.

"Tell me about Zozobra and how that all works."

He laughed in a mischievous way and smiled, "I'm not into that at all."

"Oh, too touristy; I get it."

"No, that's not it. Really, I shouldn't talk about it. You should go. It's interesting, lots of people; the city makes a bunch of money. It's all good."

"What? Is there something more I should know? I just happened across this, I've never heard of it before, and I'd like to know more."

I wanted to hear his take on it.

"You mean you didn't come here for the Fiesta?" he asked.

"Nope."

"Do you know what the Fiesta is all about?"

"Sort of; I looked it up on Google after I checked in."

Feeling stupid, I quickly added, "give me your thoughts on it."

He laughed.

"Why not. Well, there is a lot of controversy and I try to stay out of it, because I get really pissed off. I had to let it go a while back. It started back in the 1700's really, even earlier. It's a whole scene between the Native people and the Spaniards. The Native people were living here for a long time, then the Spaniards came along and took over the land and the government and killed a lot of the Natives - a real bloodbath. The Fiesta is celebrating the Spanish conquering the Natives. Plus, there is a whole bunch of religious stuff added to the mix. So, it's still sort of a Spanish versus Native thing. The whole Fiesta, to me, represents conflict and I don't think that should be celebrated. That's just my personal opinion. And there's a lot of people who feel the same. The Zozobra thing was added in as an interesting twist and really had nothing to do with the Fiesta."

"Well, that puts a new light on it." I said naively.

Since I had just heard about the whole thing an hour or so earlier I wasn't sure what to think, but I had a sense this kid was right.

He continued, "there have been some demonstrators the last few years. You'll probably see some today around the Plaza. The Fiesta committee likes to keep that to a minimum. Now, the whole Zozobra thing, that's a mad house. People everywhere. I try to stay far away from that! There's a spot up on the hill that I used to go to watch him burn. You can see pretty well, and you don't have to be part of the crowds. I don't go anymore; I stay home. But, honestly, you should go; it's something to see and you won't forget."

By that time, we had reached the shuttle drop off.

"Here we are," he said. "I'll be back here at 10 minutes to the hour, on the hour, every hour until 9 pm when you're ready to come back."

"Great," I said as I stepped out of the van.

"Have fun!" he shouted as I closed the door.

He drove off into traffic. As the van passed, the view of the Plaza opened up, and the first thing I saw was a man holding a sign. His back was to me, so I couldn't read what it said, but I didn't need to. Suddenly, I had a new view on things.

As I walked around the Plaza, I couldn't help thinking about the conversation I had just had. There was pain hidden in this city, just like Gallup, but not so easily seen. Santa Fe was a mecca for artists and writers. The architecture, the galleries, jewelry stores, world-class dining, five-star hotels, made this a tourist haven. After all, this is why I was here. I began to wonder why I somehow ended up being the only passenger in the hotel shuttle with a young man who decided to tell me that story. My mind was working overtime trying to separate my original intention for being here - art, fun, culture, jewelry, with the information and experiences that had come my way since arriving in New Mexico. I decided that I was overthinking and it was time to step out of that paradigm and begin my Santa Fe adventure as a "touristo."

But that was not to be, at least not yet. I discovered a very unique little shop down a narrow stone alley. The alley opened up into a lush garden area with an outdoor restaurant at the center. There were little twinkle lights in all the trees, and you could tell this place would look magical after dark. Along the side was a row of small shops in ancient looking adobes. One of them grabbed my attention, and I climbed the two massive stone steps and went through the carved wooden screen door. The place was about 12 feet by 12 feet and filled to the brim with jewelry, hats, and scarves. I started looking around and realized there was no one here, no salesperson. It felt a little awkward, but I just kept looking. After about 10 minutes, a young girl came through the door breathlessly.

"Hi, so sorry, I had to use the bathroom and it's in the other building," she announced.

"No problem," I said. "I'm just looking around."

"Anything special? I could give you a good price, pay no attention to the prices on the tags. My boss isn't here, but she gives me room to deal," she said with a wink.

There was something about her that felt comfortable and spirited. She just didn't seem to fit in with this store.

In one display case I saw a couple of rings that looked interesting, so I asked to see them. I tried them on, and she gave me the prices, much lower than marked, just as she said. Neither of them fit, and they were the only ones in the shop.

"This artist is from Albuquerque. If you really like it, I can give you the name of a shop that carries her stuff. Maybe you can find one in your size there," she offered.

"Thanks, but I'll keep looking. This town is filled with so much stuff, I'm sure I'll find something."

"That's for sure. Especially Friday there will be all sorts of vendors on the street for the Fiesta, and most of them make everything themselves. It's nice to buy directly from the artist," she shared.

"Great! I am looking forward to that. I just happened into being here at the right time. I bet it's crazy busy though," I remarked.

"Yep, lots of people celebrating the Fiesta," she said in a sarcastic tone.

"You're not into the Fiesta? I just talked with someone earlier today who felt the same way, a young man. He told me there is some controversy over the whole thing."

It was like the question turned on a faucet. She started telling me about her family. Her mom was Native American, her dad Mexican. Her grandparents had been extremely unhappy about the pairing, and there was nothing but family drama over it for as long as she could remember. Her Native family members rejected the Fiesta and all it stood for, and wanted nothing to do with the celebrations or her Mexican father. But, she was half Native and half Mexican and questioned what that made her? She felt like an outsider.

"All I know is there is something wrong with all of this, the whole Fiesta. They have parades, and Spanish dancers get all dressed up, and people come from all over to watch it. No offense to you. And the whole thing is based on the Spanish taking over the land, killing the Indians, and then controlling everything! And they still do!" she stated firmly.

"And get this," she went on. "This year the 'Queen' of the Fiesta is an Indian girl. Really! I think she should get up there at the Palace of the Governors and pour a bucket of blood on the wall or over herself, and shout 'This Fiesta is built on the blood of my ancestors!' How would they like that?"

She looked at me with the question hanging in the air.

"Wow, that would be intense," I responded. "It would certainly get people's attention."

"Yeah, right. Like that would ever happen. No, the queens always think it is such an honor. Ha! I can't wait to get out of this town," she confessed.

Suddenly, I felt weird. Too much information; too much intimacy.

"Are you going away to college?" I asked.

"Yes, and I only have one year left! Thank God!"

I asked her where she was going and what she planned to study. Her demeanor changed and she happily filled me in on all the details. We had a pleasant end to our conversation. I moved towards the door.

"Enjoy your stay here," she said to me as I left the store.

"Good luck with college, and I wish you all the best," I responded as I made my way down the big stone steps and back into the courtyard.

My head was spinning a bit. I really wanted to get back into my tourist mode! What was going on? This was much more than I wanted to know about Santa Fe.

As I walked back into the Plaza, I was transported. It was a feeling of being sent back in time. I imagined dirt roads and Native people in their Native wear walking the sidewalks. Spaniards on horses, clip clopping through the streets. Horse drawn wagons filled with supplies. Kids playing in the park at the center of the square. I took a deep breath and smelled food cooking, and it was bringing me back to reality. It was late afternoon and I hadn't eaten since early morning at the hotel; I was starving. Within a few yards I found the source of the enticing smells, a small cafe. Its sign announced it has been on the square since 1949. I went in and was given a great spot right by the big front windows overlooking the Plaza. The lunch was fantastic; I enjoyed every bite and even bought a piece of pie to go.

Afterwards I sat relaxing, contemplating what I had learned from the two young people I had encountered and enjoying the view from my window booth. There was a lot to see here. So, I decided to spend the rest of the afternoon combing my way through the shops that surrounded the Plaza and the Native street vendors who had their wares on blankets on the sidewalk. Thoughts of Native New Mexicans being conquered and killed by the Spaniards were pushed to the back of my mind.

There were several couples at the shuttle pick-up spot when I arrived, so I knew it was coming soon. I was ready to get back to the hotel and take a rest before I went to watch the sunset at the park across the street from the hotel. Nothing I liked better than a good sunset. Every day and every place you go it's different. Something about watching a sunset connects me to something bigger; it has ever since I was a little girl. I was jarred out of my thoughts as the shuttle pulled up to the curb. It was the same young man driving, and I chose the front seat again.

"How was your day?" he asked.

"Interesting." I responded as the couples loaded up. "Remember what we were talking about this morning?"

"Yes," he looked at me tentatively. "We can't talk about that now." His head slightly nodded towards the back, towards the other passengers.

"Oh, okay," I said, a little annoyed.

"It just that the hotel doesn't like me talking about that stuff. People come here to have fun and enjoy the celebrations." He spoke quietly, almost in a whisper.

"I get it. Not good for business. Well, I just wanted to tell you that I met a young woman in a shop who has the same beliefs as you and I learned a lot. Thank you for being honest with me this morning. It gives me a whole new perspective."

He smiled and nodded at me. We rode the rest of the way back to the hotel in silence. It didn't take long. When he stopped, I slid down from the high seat in the big van and walked away towards my room.

"Have a nice night. See you tomorrow," the driver shouted at me as I crossed the parking lot.

I waved my hand towards him.

"Yeah, see you tomorrow," I said softly as I dug in my purse for the room key.

"Burn Him! Burn Him!"

"I try not to worry about the future - so I take each day just one anxiety attack at a time." - Tom Wilson

It was Thursday, Zozobra day! It occurred to me that since I couldn't find a way to put my "glooms" in Zozobra that I could at least write things down that I wanted to release and do it virtually. So, I got my laptop, brewed a cup of coffee, made myself comfortable, and started writing a list.

- Release my obsession with my weight and the shame I have been living under over gaining 80 pounds.
- Release my need to prove something - to myself, my family, the world at large. I no longer wanted to feel like I needed to "be" something or do something to feel I have value.
- Release the need to please. To stop saying "yes" when I wanted to say "no". And, instead learn to speak my own truth.
- Release the need to keep fixing myself. Looking outside myself for answers that I knew I could only find inside. (Already there waiting for me.) I must stop buying self-help books, taking classes, seeking wholeness where it was unavailable.

- Release the poverty mentality. The "make-do" belief system I had lived with most of my life that was holding me hostage in a cycle of doing without. Keeping me feeling "less than."
- Release the self-sabotage that has dictated my life since I could remember. Always attacking when I was near the completion of something I felt was important.
- Mostly, I wanted to release judgment. Judgment of myself and others. It was the cornerstone of my life. I had grown up always aware of the question, "What would people think?" I didn't know who those people were, but I knew they were judging me. I learned to judge myself by that invisible standard, and to quickly judge others as a means of self-defense. It was time to stop living the craziness of this outwardly focused life.

I stopped for a moment and read the list. That was a lot of crap. I imagined my life if I could really stuff that in Zozobra and have it be gone from my life forever! Tonight, that could happen! Then I could wake up tomorrow and feel like a new person. I daydreamed for a while about how that would feel. My heart raced a bit, feeling excited and anxious. The physical sensations snapped me back into reality. I read the list again. Yes, that was enough for Zozobra to handle. If I could let go of this list, life would be pretty damn good. Now, I just had to figure out how to send this all virtually to him when I got there tonight.

The burning of Zozobra didn't begin until 9 pm, so I had the entire day to see more of Santa Fe. After the day I had at the Plaza yesterday, I definitely wanted to head somewhere else.

I got out the Visitor's Guide and started planning my day. Reviewing all the choices, and there were a lot, I chose Canyon Road Galleries, the Museum of International Folk Art, the Santa Fe School of Cooking, and an art supply store called Artisan that a woman had told me about the day before. If that didn't fill up the day, I knew I could easily find something else.

The map on my iPhone was programmed, and I took off. The first stop, Canyon Road. It wasn't too far from my hotel, and it was a beautiful drive. Since it was Thursday, and mid-morning, the traffic was light. When I arrived at Canyon Road, I wasn't sure what to expect, but found a narrow street with small houses and adobes that had been turned into art galleries. There was parking on the street, but I worried if cars could get by; it was really narrow and also a one-way street. I saw a few other cars parked, so I pulled over close to the curb and hoped for the best.

I wasn't sure where to start. It looked very quiet, and I only saw a couple of people walking down the street; I wondered if they were open. I looked both ways, and decided to follow my gut and pick the first shop that appealed to me. Just a few buildings down the street was an adobe with blue trim, big pots filled with beautiful plants, and a huge colorful painting hanging on an outside wall. The two big front doors were open. This was the one. I walked in. It was filled with beautiful paintings, a calm, peaceful environment, with gentle music wafting through the air. I felt myself sigh, and I was starting to enjoy this day.

For the next couple of hours, I took in the sights of Canyon Road. There were a few shops where I had found things to buy, and was happy I had money to spend. These little items would be nice mementos of my time here, and I also bought a couple of gifts. However, as time passed I was subtly feeling myself get more and more uncomfortable. People had begun appearing along the road and in the galleries. Some of them locals, you could tell, other tourists like me, but *not* like me. They were obviously people with real money. There was business going on with the gallery staff and, what I guessed were, interior designers. From conversations, I overheard it seemed they were picking up art for clients. This was all very upscale.

My uncomfortable feelings started to turn into something more, as I started feeling totally out of place. My "less-than" complex was kicking in. This anxious part of me that popped up from time to time was showing up, and I felt like they were looking at me with judgment and questioning what I was doing there. The little critical voice in my head was taking this and running with it. I left the shop I was in and walked outside, trying to regain some composure, but then was confronted with people on the sidewalks.

I noticed that most of the people were older, baby boomer types and couples. They all looked so happy, in love even, having a wonderful time. All dressed very nicely, looking healthy and affluent. My stomach flipped, and I felt my heartbeat increase. One couple passed me on the sidewalk and it felt like they didn't move at all, like I was invisible. It was a very narrow sidewalk, and I had to step into the street. I could feel the heat grow up from the neck and flood my face, perspiration started to bead on my forehead.

"Stop it!" I said to myself. "You have as much right to be here as anybody."

But that crazy, worthless part of me wouldn't hear it. I took a few deep breaths and found a spot under a tree, where the sidewalk widened, and stopped.

"Get a grip," I chastised myself.

The breathing was helping, but I could feel the panic setting in down low in my gut. This had happened before, unfortunately. This time I decided it would be different. So, I forced myself to keep walking and tried to shift my focus.

Up ahead I saw a unique little garden area with some crazy painted garden poles, the colors were bright and wild. This seemed more like my kind of place. The colors distracted me, thankfully, and I began to try to figure out what the poles were made of and how. They were tall, at least six or seven feet tall. They looked like painted metal sculptures, but then I thought they might be PVC pipe, interesting.

Just then a woman came out of the open door to the gallery attached to the garden. I turned to look at her.

"Is there something I can do for you?" she asked in a bored, kind of snotty way.

"No, just looking around. Thanks," I said back, trying to sound confident. But feeling very self-conscious, especially of my weight. I suddenly felt like a beached whale.

She let out a big sigh, and went back inside, her blond hair flipped over her shoulder. She was beautiful and dressed so cool, she looked like something out of a Santa Fe Living Magazine. Her "coolness" was so apparent.

I was flooded with another old familiar feeling, envy. What must it be like to look like that! What was I thinking when I saw these bright colored towers? I thought there must be some cool, funky, outsider artist inside, that was bucking the norm on this seemingly pretentious street. But no, just another person to push my panic button and set off my self-esteem and self-consciousness issues. I had to get out of here. My car was blocks away and the crowds had grown heavier. I sensed that I was about to elevate this insecurity attack to a fight or flight level and if I didn't get to my car and quick, who knows what would happen.

I started walking in a purposeful stance, hoping I looked like I had somewhere to go and I knew where it was. But instead, I was looking at the people, feeling hot, fat, self-conscious, and wishing I was anywhere but here. My clothes seemed to get tighter; I was starting to sweat. I imagined my stomach sticking out and my big butt getting bigger and bigger. It was like a scene from a movie about a psychotic person. It was about to the point where I imagined people stopping in their tracks pointing at me and laughing that I reached the car.

Thank God! I had never been so happy to see that blue car in my life. I unlocked the door, jumped in, started the engine, cranked on the air conditioner, and started to cry. What in the hell is the matter with me?

It took me a few minutes to compose myself; I felt safe in my car. The wave of craziness seemed to be passing, and I was beginning to feel normal again. I was left feeling exhausted and hungry. Food, yes, that's what I need. I had to get out of here and find something to eat. The story of my life. Using food to soothe. But I was hungry; it had been hours since I ate. Normal people eat food! I persuaded myself. But deep inside I had the feeling that I didn't deserve to eat, especially after the scene I had just survived. Being fat was my "crazy." If I could just stop eating, maybe the crazy would go away.

Numbly, I drove around looking for a place I could eat and not have the panic attack re-start. I picked a couple of places, but changed my mind. I finally settled on an Indian place. It was dark, quiet, and had a lunch buffet. I could eat quickly and get out of there.

Afterwards, I forced myself to go to the art supply store, Artisan. Thankfully it wasn't far, but there was nothing there that really excited me. I was feeling pretty down, and being alone with my thoughts was really making it worse. Usually art supplies affect me like a drug, a real jolt of energy, but not today. I left empty handed. All I wanted to do was get back to the Sage Inn, close the drapes, and crawl into bed, even though it was the middle of the afternoon. I got back in the car and drove directly to the hotel. I closed the drapes, put on my pajamas, and got under the covers.

*　*　*

When I started to wake up, it was nearly six o'clock. I got up from bed and sat on the edge for a minute. My head hurt and my eyes were blurry. What had happened, why did I let myself go crazy like that? I took a big deep breath, got up, and opened the drapes. Bright light flooded the room, and I could see the shuttle and people milling around it near the front entrance to the hotel. A direct view. I realized that I had better get it together and get ready for the night's adventure to see Zozobra burn. The shuttle would be filling up quickly every hour, and I needed to get there and find a good vantage point. I headed for the shower.

One of the main things I had been looking forward to on this trip was having time alone to think and process all the stuff that was going on at this stage of my life. For the past three years I was living back in my hometown, the same one I had left as soon as I turned 18 and never looked back. I had moved back to help out my parents, who were 89 and 93. Never totally thinking through what living in the desert would mean (I always hated it) or what being around them would bring up (they had no idea who I am). Plus, I was in a marriage that was far from perfect, and I was feeling stifled in a very big way. There was a part of me, the girl who loved to create fantasy, who imagined driving off on this adventure and never going back, just starting a new life. This "mini" breakdown I had today brought all that front and center. It contained elements of all my issues wrapped into one event. Especially the throat chakra issues, not speaking my truth, saying yes when I really wanted to say no, not feeling known, wanting to please people, not to mention all the self-worth and esteem issues. This was all coming to a head, and it wasn't pretty. Just three days alone with my own thoughts, and I was going nuts.

The hot water felt good, and I began to feel better. I imagined all the issues of the day and the ones I wanted to send to Zozobra vanishing down the drain with the water, flowing through the pipes, and somehow ending up at Fort Mercy Park, magically floating up into Zozobra. It felt good to release it all.

Once dressed and ready I went to the window again. It was nearly 7 pm and there was a large crowd waiting for the shuttle. I was planning on taking this one, but the thought of being packed like sardines in the van brought up unpleasant memories of the incident on Canyon Road. I didn't want to do it. Right then I decided I wasn't going. No way. The people in the shuttle, and then all the people at the park, no way. I would stay in my nice cozy hotel room and watch TV. It was settled. I took off my shoes and sat on the bed, piling pillows behind my back, and clicked the remote. The news flashed on, and they were covering the events at Fort Mercy Park. It was the Albuquerque news, with a reporter "live" from the park. He was talking about the crowds, and the camera panned the field, which was a sea of people, then up towards the gigantic figure of Zozobra. He talked about the weather being perfect, no wind. The excitement in the air at the 89th burning of Mr. Gloom.

Oh crap, I thought. I can't sit here. I have to go! How would I feel tomorrow morning if I didn't go? I asked myself. I clicked off the TV and got up from the bed. I put on my shoes, grabbed my purse, my phone, and the map of downtown Santa Fe, and rushed out to get in the shuttle. Luckily, my seat in the front was open and I got in.

"Ready for the big event?" asked the young driver.

"As ready as I'll ever be," I responded from my shotgun seat.

Someone from the back asked, "Do you have any suggestions about where we should watch?"

"Well, Zozobra is up higher than the people so he's easy to see from most anywhere. But I suggest not going over the bridges. It gets crazy trying to leave. There are only three walking bridges that go in to the main park area, and it gets really crowded when all those people are trying to get out at the same time," he shared.

"And remember, the shuttle stops running at nine, so if you want a ride, be at the pick-up spot. You're on your own after that."

Since the burning didn't start until after nine, it was likely none of us would be at the pick-up spot. I was glad I had my map. And, I was really glad to know about the walking bridges. Just then, the van slowed down.

"Here we are folks. It's still a ways to go, but the roads are all closed and I can't go any further. You'll have to walk from here. Just follow the crowds."

We thanked him, and all got off the shuttle. In every direction you looked, there were flocks of people walking through the city streets. All you had to do was pick a street and follow someone. Which is exactly what I did. A nice family with a couple kids and a baby in a stroller. They looked like locals who knew their way around. It was a good choice. We weaved through the streets, passing through the Plaza and then onto a big wide street that had been closed to traffic, and the entire road was filled with people walking towards the park. I followed the herd. There were thousands of people. It was crazy! As I walked, I noticed there were not too many people walking alone. There were groups of kids, families, couples, all sorts of combinations. I was starting to get that uncomfortable feeling, but talked myself out of it and moved forward.

At the top of the street the road sort of merged into the park and there I got my first real full view of Zozobra. Wow, was all I could think. Wow! He was enormous! He was tethered up on a small rise near the field and was lighted from the inside; he seemed to glow. He was huge; it looked like he was more than 50 feet tall. His big arms and hands were waving in the air; his fingers pointing to the crowds. His face was very scary looking, and it seemed like fire was coming out of his eyes. This was an amazing sight.

As far as I could see there were people everywhere. I realized that most for these people must have been here for hours to get places up close. I stopped for a moment to orient myself and from this vantage point I could see the three bridges that our driver had told us about. Most of the people were there, across the bridges and in the big field at the base of the rise. Thousands and thousands of them. Luckily, it was a big sports complex and the field on this side of the bridges was huge; that is where I would head, but I could see that area was filling up quickly too. People were pushing around me, so I moved with the crowd toward the ticket tent. This was one crazy event, and people had come from all over. I never could have imagined this.

I managed to get my ticket and lined up to go through the turnstiles. Once in the park, I tried to find a good viewing area. It was still difficult to get my head around all the people and the excitement in the air. There was a pavilion at the center of the field that sold souvenirs of all sorts, and pushcarts with luminescent glow sticks, necklaces, and wands, plus lots of other kid- friendly items. All of them 20 deep with people trying to buy something. Off to the left was a row of tents serving food, all of which had long lines too. I saw one serving Indian tacos, and I walked over, got in line, and waited.

Taco in hand, I went to find a place to sit with a good view. There was a short cement wall, and I found a spot near a couple of families. It was only 7:45 pm, and the burning didn't start until nine. I settled in, ate my taco, and did some people watching. It was quite interesting. More and more people were streaming in the gates, most of them crossing the bridges. There was standing room only in that area, and I was so glad our driver had warned us about that. I felt much more calm and comfortable being further away and closer to the exit. The noise level started to rise and the feeling of excitement grew. I had never seen or experienced anything like this before. It was exhilarating, yet I also had a sense of it being really weird. All these people waiting to burn up an effigy. Strange, to say the least.

Suddenly, there was a loud groaning sound coming through the giant speakers around the park. People responded immediately, clapping, yelling, hooting. The groans got louder and louder, and I realized Old Man Gloom had come to life and was moaning and groaning at the crowds below him. The lights went out and the only light in the place was focused on Zozobra. His body was weaving around, his giant fingers raised up pointing at the crowd with a "shame on you" kind of action. The crowd was going nuts. The moans got creepier, louder, and seemed a bit scary. It felt like this giant monster was chastising us all. It was a cross between angry groans and someone in pain. It was hard to tell, but it was loud and the people loved it.

A few minutes passed and the place went dark again. This time Zozobra went dark as well. Then the tether lines holding him up started lighting up and became a stream of fireworks as they moved up the lines, a shower of sparks high above the crowds. I was thinking this must be it, the fireworks are going to move up the ropes and set him on fire, but no, they stopped midway. A group of fire dancers appeared on the hill near him, and drummers started pounding drums. The crowds roared. The place was going crazy. The music got louder. The dancers performed a synchronized routine, and it was beautiful. My skin felt tingly. The drumbeat was so loud and ferocious it filled the entire area, making the hairs on the back of my neck rise. Electric. Even more dancers flooded out, more music, more instruments; it was a full sensual experience.

Meanwhile, Zozobra is still groaning in the background, faster and louder, and you could sense this was coming to a climax soon.

There was a young couple standing near me, and they had a little boy about three years old. He was on his dad's shoulders. I looked at him and he was half smiling, half crying, and every few seconds he looked down at his mom for reassurance. She smiled up at him and that seemed to keep him feeling like this was okay and normal. As I watched, I was thinking, what must be going on in his mind? A little kid witnessing this scene. What happens when they go home and he goes to bed? This was nightmare-producing stuff. This was the weirdest thing I had ever witnessed, and the weirdest part was yet to come.

With the music pounding, the dancers in a frenzy, and Zozobra moaning and waving his giant index fingers all over the place, the crowd was going wild.

Somewhere in the big field, some people started shouting, "BURN HIM! BURN HIM!"

Before long the voices of the crowd overpowered the moans and the music, and it was a mass of noise with the chanting of "burn him" reverberating in the complex.

It was mesmerizing, yet freaky and crazy. Everyone was caught up in the frenzy. I was trying to remember that this was about letting go of the past and burning him was part of the ritual, but another part of me was thinking this is mob mentality and there is a possibility of things going really bad here. But what? I had no idea. All these people just wanted to burn Zozobra and start the new year fresh. Cries from the little boy on his dad's shoulders got my attention, and I watched as the dad handed him off to the mom who was now holding him close. You could tell he felt safer half buried in his mom's neck, yet turning to watch the craziness in front of us.

With the crowd shouting, "burn him," the drummers pounding the drums, and the fire dancers began to form a circle around the effigy, it was getting close.

The crowd felt it and the chanting got louder and faster, "burn him! Burn him! Burn him!"

The dancers filed off, leaving one lone dancer holding a huge, long torch. He moved it towards the base of Zozobra, the flame jumped, and then the entire base was set on fire. Somewhere from inside, Zozobra fireworks began to go off and he was engulfed in flames.

Zozobra started to groan louder and faster than before. The people were going absolutely nuts! From behind him another set of fireworks started to go off; these were 4th of July kind of fireworks, big, high, and lots of them, just like a fireworks finale. It was unbelievable.

Zozobra started moaning again. This time as he was almost entirely engulfed in flames, his arms flailing around as the fire burned him up. It took only minutes for him to be totally torched. He began to collapse.

Before long he was a pile of charred rubble, while in the background the people cheered and fireworks were still going off in the sky.

It had all been so wild and crazy and quick that I hadn't even thought about sending my issues to him virtually. I visualized them zooming through the air and being thrown on top of the pile of smoldering Zozobra, and I let them go.

Within seconds of the burn, people were already heading out. It was as if everyone suddenly knew it was going to be an ordeal to get out, and they wanted to make a quick exit. Ha! The turnstiles we all had used to enter had been removed, and it was an open path out of the park. Thousands of people were moving towards that area, and it was gridlock. Thankfully I was close, so I made it out much quicker than I expected. Once out of the park, the road opened up and I started my trek back to the hotel. The streets were filled with people going in every direction. It was after 10:30 pm, and it was at least a mile or so to the hotel. Within a few blocks the crowds had dissipated, and I was suddenly aware of being alone on the dark, quiet streets of Santa Fe. After another few blocks it was eerily still, the occasional car driving past. There were sounds of people still celebrating far off in the distance.

It felt a bit scary, and I became painfully aware of being all alone. It seemed so strange to have been part of that huge mass of people, and now be nearly alone on the quiet streets. A couple of blocks ahead, I spotted a couple walking hand in hand. They looked like tourists. Quickening my pace, I caught up with them and hung a few yards behind. Just being near them felt safer. We walked together the rest of the way, until we reached the intersection near my hotel. They turned right, and I crossed the street.

I sent them an energetic "thank you," and quickly crossed the parking lot towards my hotel. At that moment, I felt a huge sense of relief. What an amazing thing I had just witnessed. It was hard to process it all, but I knew it had been a gift. My body was tired, but still on an adrenaline rush from the walk home and the wild scene at Fort Mercy Park. My mind was still trying to make sense of it all. My feet were killing me by the time I reached my door. I slid my key card in the slot and the green light clicked. I opened the door and took a big sigh of relief. Once inside I quickly brushed my teeth, put on my pajamas, and fell into bed. I was so glad I went; it was something I will never forget. I lay there, thinking about it all. Part of me could hardly believe I had just witnessed what I had witnessed. And, it had been happening for 89 years! As I drifted off to sleep I was wondering if I would wake up feeling different in the morning, a fresh new clean year ahead, thanks to Zozobra's sacrifice.

FIESTAS DE SANTA FE
JEWELRY, FOOD, AND MAGIC

"Santa Fe is the artiest, sculpturest, weaviest and potteryest town on earth." - Jan Morris

My final morning in Santa Fe. Today was the day I had been waiting 10 years for - the first day of the Painting from Your Wild Heart Retreat! I didn't have to be there until dinnertime, so I had most of the day to finish seeing the sights I had planned. Plus, today was the beginning of the Fiestas de Santa Fe and I knew the streets of the Plaza would be filled with vendors of all types.

Thankfully, I was feeling refreshed and looking forward to the day ahead. The panic attack I had had the day before seemed like history. I lay in bed for a few minutes thinking about Zozobra and the walk home and it seemed nearly like a dream. But, somehow, I did feel better, with renewed vigor and a better attitude. Maybe I had begun a new, clean, fresh year!

It didn't take me long to get ready, and I headed to the hotel lobby for a quick breakfast. The shuttle was there and "my" driver was waiting. It was the first run of the day and I wanted to get to the Plaza early, before all the crowds. Just a few people got on the shuttle, and we took off. When we turned the corner near our drop off spot, I could see the area had been transformed, the streets closed to traffic, filled with tents and pop-ups, and people milling around getting their booths in order. This was going to be fun. I wanted to buy some jewelry from a local artist; that was my mission today.

It took no time at all to find something I wanted to buy. I spotted a beautiful coral and turquoise necklace with a unique silver clasp. The woman selling it was about my age and looked so content and peaceful. I was immediately drawn to her.

"Did you find something you like?" she asked me.

"Oh yes," I responded. "This coral necklace; I love it."

"That is a nice one, I have to say," she said with a coy, yet confident smile.

"I agree. I'll take it," I laughed.

It was so nice to hear someone speak so honestly and confidently about their own work.

"How long have you been making jewelry?" I asked.

"Well, since I was a little girl really. But I didn't start taking it seriously until about six years ago."

She went on to tell me about working in San Francisco in the business world for years and hating it, but accepting it as her life. She was hooked into the whole mindset - work, benefits, 401K, retirement, etc.

"The worker bee syndrome," she called it.

"Then, a friend invited me to come to Santa Fe for a visit. She'd visited here, loved it, quit her job, and moved here. I remember thinking she was crazy when she did it. It took me nearly six years to make it here for a visit. Isn't that sad?"

She shook her head.

"Anyway, once I was here I fell in love. Something shifted in me and I realized there was a different way to live, and I wanted it. So, I did it. I got up my nerve, gave my notice, sold my house, and moved to Santa Fe. My family thought I was crazy!"

She laughed a sweet, knowing kind of laugh.

"Now they think it's the smartest thing I ever did."

"Do you live downtown?" I asked.

"Oh, no. Believe it or not, I live about 10 miles from town, just north of here. I have a very small house that I absolutely love, and a really nice studio that I had built. It's perfect. I don't have cable or internet, just me living at peace and making jewelry."

"Wow, no internet, no website? How can you sell your jewelry?" I asked.

"The old-fashioned way," she smiled. "Person to person, just like this. Plus, I have my stuff in a few shops around town."

We chatted a while longer, and she wrapped up my necklace. There was something about this woman that gave me hope, yet frightened me. The thought of not having internet access just sent shivers up and down my spine. How could you live in the 21st century and not be "connected"?

But yet, I wanted some of what she had. The letting go; the surrender to her passion. Especially the choosing a life she loved, rather than being stuck in a place she didn't want to be. Plus, her aura just radiated with calm, serenity, and a subtle joy that felt like a warm embrace. Yes, this woman had something I wanted, and she was a messenger. Something had brought us together this beautiful morning, and I was very glad. She handed me the bag.

"It's been so nice talking to you," I said.

"Thanks. I don't know what got over me; I told you my whole life story," she laughed. "But, I know there is a reason for everything. Enjoy your necklace. It was made with love while I was looking out over this glorious land. There is heart in it."

She looked at me with knowingness.

"Thank you. When I wear it, I'll remember that, and you, too."

We smiled at each other, and I walked away. Somehow, I knew that I was done here. I didn't need to do anymore shopping at the Fiesta. I had gotten what I came for.

*   *   *

The Santa Fe School of Cooking was not far from the Plaza, so I got out my map, found its location, and started off in that direction. I wasn't sure what to expect, but I had found it online several months ago and "liked" them on Facebook and had been reading their posts for weeks. It seemed like a happening spot.

On my way, I passed a sign for the Georgia O'Keeffe Museum, which reminded me I wanted to go there too. I had been before, years ago, but since I was going to the place where she lived I thought it would be good to see it again and get re-acquainted with her story.

The streets of Santa Fe are like nowhere else. The architecture, the unique style, and the narrow streets made it seem like an adventure just walking around. It had a great feeling that I loved.

It wasn't long before I found the cooking school. It was in an old building with a grid of glass windows instead of the regular plate glass ones. It looked warm, friendly, and inviting. The doorbell rang as I entered. It opened onto a little shop where they sold all kinds of wares and New Mexico cookbooks. The actual cooking school part was behind a set of doors. It was fun just being there. I imagined what it must be like to be a local and take classes. Actually, I had seen pictures on Facebook and I really wished there was something like it close to where I lived. The best part of being there was the feeling I had. It was a realization that cooking and making food was fun. All the gadgets, accessories, the cookbooks, the utensils. All of it reminded me of the joy of cooking.

At that moment, I realized that I had given that up years ago. Some part of me only saw food as "good" or "bad" and that spending too much time around food would lead to gaining more weight. My mindset had become, make it, eat it, get it over with. It had become a chore, and I had become completely disconnected from food. Too many years depriving myself or feeling guilty about eating had turned me off of cooking as fun. This shop was waking me up. Internally I had known that when I first found their Facebook page. There was a part of me that was drawn to the pictures of people in aprons, laughing, chopping, tasting food together, drinking wine, and connecting around food. I wanted that in my life. It seemed robust and sensual, living fully and savoring life and food, eating and drinking. What could be wrong with that? Some long ago pushed away part of me was coming alive in this shop. It felt good; actually, it felt great! Something was happening, and I liked it. My heart and my mind were opening up to seeing things differently. Maybe I had been wrong; yes, I had been wrong. That rigid part of me, the one raised by a Marine, had that military value of black and white thinking entrenched in my psyche. It was all or nothing.

With food, I had let go of the joy long ago and put it in the "nothing" category, seeing it as an enemy to be avoided or an indulgence to feel shame and remorse about. Somehow, I had been drawn to this shop for this very reason. It was time to open my mind and my heart again to the joy of food. This was feeling good.

There was a part of me that felt like I had to buy something to remind me of this revelation, a talisman of sort. But as I looked at all the items for sale, it became clear to me that coming here was enough. What this place had awakened in me couldn't be forgotten. A new door had been opened, and like Pandora's box, it could never be closed again. It was big, huge! On the most basic level, food and nutrition are life giving. There is life in food, and joy in it. It was time I found that again!

As I left the shop, my mind was sifting through all the experiences I had had, people I had met, and things I had seen in Santa Fe. It seemed like a scavenger hunt, finding clues in various locations, learning things about myself, and opening up to new ideas. I wasn't sure what was happening, but I was paying attention.

As I walked back towards the Square, my eye spotted something in a shop window and I stopped to take a look. It was jewelry, but not like anything I had seen so far in Santa Fe. This was unusual, more like found objects assembled into amazing treasures. I had to go in! It was a very small shop, not much bigger than a small bedroom. In the corner was a traditional kiva fireplace with a big hearth, and sitting on the hearth was an old man. He looked like he had seen things, been places. He fit this place. Dressed in khaki hiking shorts with lots of pockets, earthy sandals, and an open neck sweatshirt. Several necklaces with turquoise hung around his neck along with a lanyard connected to his reading glasses. On his wrist was an amazing old vintage bracelet, similar to those in the window. His hair was stark white, and he had a well-grown soul patch beneath his bottom lip.

"Hello there," he said. "Come in and look around."

"Thanks," I responded, and I went towards the lone jewelry case.

"My daughter makes that jewelry. Interesting stuff. Me, I paint; my stuff is over there."

He pointed to the wall and a couple of shelves.

"Thanks," I repeated myself, not sure what to say.

"Where you from? You here for the Fiesta?" he asked.

"California. No, I just happened across all this. I'm heading to the Ghost Ranch for a retreat and thought I would take a couple of extra days to explore Santa Fe."

"Oh, Abiquiu. Yes, the Ghost Ranch. It's so beautiful out there. Nothing like it. There is something about that land out there.

Definitely something special. I head out there occasionally to make paper, I know a guy who lives in Abiquiu and we make it together. Are you taking a painting class?"

"Sort of," I responded. "It's an intuitive painting retreat called Painting from the Wild Heart. I'm not sure what it is really, but I know it's not an average painting class."

He laughed a Santa Claus sort of belly laugh, which made me smile and feel warmly comforted.

"Yes, that doesn't sound like an average painting class. You do know painting can heal you, don't you?" he quizzed.

"Absolutely. That's why I am going. I have a lot of things I want to heal, and I am tired of trying to figure it out in my head. Thought I'd let my creative spirit work on it instead," I confessed.

"Smart girl."

He smiled and gave a low chuckle.

This guy was interesting and seemed very wise. I moved away from the jewelry and started looking at his paintings. They were all very small. He must have sensed the question in my mind.

"They are all small because I paint on the road and these fit in my backpack. I've painted all over the world. Last year I spent three months in the Australian outback. So, small works for me, plus I get to capture things in a different way. I see things differently."

I had a stack of his small paintings in my hand and he started telling me about them, what they were, where he had painted them. Each one had a story. I came across one of two fish in the most beautiful shades of blue and green. The colors resonated with me, brilliant peacock blue, sea glass aqua, and bright lime green on a stark white background.

"I have to have this one. I love it!"

"I painted that one in Greece."

Then he told me the story.

I loved listening to him and the amazing stories of his life as an artist. His name was Ross and he seemed to live his life following his passion for painting and adventure. He took the painting from me and moved to a small table, where he began to wrap it up in an old city map.

"Tell me more about this retreat you're going to?" he asked as he worked.

I told him my story of wanting to go for 10 years, but never allowing myself. How my friends had pushed me and I finally signed up. I shared how I had always been a process painter, making art to work through difficult emotional times, or to memorialize some event. I told him what I had read about Painting from the Wild Heart on the web and what I expected it might be. As he was finishing up, I saw him write something on the outside of the package.

"What's that?" I asked.

"Something I want you to remember," he answered. "I wrote, Painting is to love again . . . to love yourself. That's what you're going to find out. That's what painting will do for you. It's time."

He handed me the package. I smiled. He smiled. I wasn't sure what to say, so I thanked him and turned to leave. I was just about out the door when he said.

"Enjoy the drive to the Ghost Ranch. There is magic out there; don't miss it!"

I smiled at him again as I left the shop. He waved, with a mischievous grin. I felt a bit like Alice in Wonderland. Had I fallen down some rabbit hole on the way to New Mexico? I kept running into such interesting people who seemed to be telling me things that I needed to hear, going places that made me feel things I needed to feel. It was strange. I wasn't entirely sure what to make of it all.

My last stop before leaving town was the Georgia O'Keeffe Museum. It wasn't too far away and I was there within minutes. It was a busy day, being Fiesta, and lots of people filled the rooms. A docent was giving a talk in the big gallery, so I went there to listen. She was telling the story of Georgia's early life and her love affair with Alfred Stieglitz, the photographer. She had copies of letters they wrote to each other. She talked about her first gallery show put on by Stieglitz in New York. She also described Georgia's early paintings of the skyline of New York, which seemed so strange and dark.

After a few minutes, I walked away. I just wanted to look at the art and get myself in the mood for my journey to the Ghost Ranch. In the quiet of the rooms I transported myself into history and imagined Georgia alone, painting in her beloved desert. Her mind on the painting and the process, never thinking about who would buy it, where it would be shown, none of that. It was something that flowed from her, like breath, part the painting, part the land, part the spirit that it held. You could feel it in her work. I would find a painting and stand in front of it for minutes, allowing myself to absorb it fully. It was easy for me to get in that place, connect with that feeling; it's why I had come. There was something sacred at the Ghost Ranch, and I wanted part of that in my life!

Near the entrance was a little theatre showing films about Georgia's life. I found a seat and watched. This part of the film was about her later and final years in Abiquiu. Perfect. It showed her painting out near the beautiful hills, taking her lunch, walking the land the entire day, cooking big pots of soup in her kitchen, and writing letters at her small desk. Her peaceful and reclusive life was chronicled in film.

I paid close attention to the surroundings and the buildings, hoping to orient myself in preparation for my arrival. Watching where she walked, the places she sat, and even the things in the background. It felt a bit surreal to know in just a few short hours I would be there, getting ready to begin this intuitive painting process. I had no idea what to expect. But after being here, watching the film, I knew it was all going to be perfect, no matter what happened. The sacred ground of the Ghost Ranch was calling.

GHOST RANCH OR BUST

"Travel far enough, you meet yourself." - David Mitchell

The shuttle stop was crowded with people. When it arrived, I took my seat in the front, feeling like it had been designated mine. It took a while to get back to the hotel, because of so many pedestrians and cars. My mind had already made the shift, and I was thinking ahead into the rest of the day. Santa Fe was beginning to feel like a foggy memory as I began to mentally plan my next step. The shuttle arrived at the hotel. I said my goodbyes to my new friend, the driver.

"Thanks for all the rides and your honesty," I said to him.

"No problem," he responded. "Are you leaving?"

"Yep, on my way to the Ghost Ranch."

"Have a good time. Be careful out there; it's pretty isolated," he warned as I waved goodbye and headed to the parking lot.

I'd already checked out and packed early, so I was ready to go. I entered the address to the Ghost Ranch in my phone, checked the screen, and realized I was close to the main road to Espanola, my next stop.

It wasn't long after leaving Santa Fe that the houses started getting fewer and fewer, and the open land of New Mexico sprawled in front of me. I was filled with excitement. This was it; I was on my way. Heading to this retreat after 10 years of wanting. Driving through this land, so scared and haunting, that had been calling me for decades. I felt extra alert and paid close attention to everything in view. I'd been told that I might lose cell phone reception once outside Santa Fe. So, I called my mom one last time to check in with her, to make sure things were okay. After today I would be off the grid, out of touch, for the next six days. The Ghost Ranch had telephone service and I had left that number, to be used for emergency only, just in case. I had decided before I came that I was unplugging everything - phone, email, Facebook, internet, all of it. It just needed to be that way.

My mom answered in her usual upbeat manner. Although she was 93, her voice was strong and her attitude spry. I asked how things were, and then told her about some of my adventures the past couple of days. Just a few minutes into the call, I lost cell coverage and she was gone. This was it; I was cut off.

AT&T had acted on my behalf and shut down my call, signaling me that it was time. Freedom arrived. It felt like my escape into this sacred journey had officially begun. I was now on my own, out of touch with the real world. This was it. From here on out, it was all about me. That felt pretty strange, yet incredibly exhilarating! I inhaled a big, deep breath and exhaled slowly, feeling my entire body relax and my mind calm down. I was ready. Yes, I was. Whatever was coming, I was going to embrace and participate fully. That was the promise I made to myself.

The landscape began to change. Hills rolled out along the sides of the road, and small mountains in interesting formations began to appear. My final stop before the Ghost Ranch was the small town of Espanola. It took over an hour to get there, and it seemed I was going further and further into the middle of nowhere. I was surprised at the size of the town, and I pulled into a market for water and some snacks for the week. It was a short stop, and then I was on my way again. Leaving Espanola, the houses became even sparser and the road narrowed to two lanes. The pavement seemed to change color. As I looked ahead, I could see more mountains and a crystal clear blue sky with a few blindingly white puffy clouds. Whiter than I had ever seen. It looked like a picture from a travel magazine. I found myself mesmerized by the land, the panoramic views, and the colors. Things had shifted, and I was embracing this connection with nature, this land of New Mexico. It was breathtaking.

Along the way I stopped at least half a dozen times to take pictures, being awed at every sloping turn. The road would stretch out for a couple of miles, and then wind around craggy mountains like I had never seen. The ribbons of colors running through them horizontally marked life on earth through the ages. Some of the towering pinnacles I remembered seeing in paintings by Georgia O'Keeffe; I recognized them right away. In every direction, the beauty of this desert filled my vision and I knew why she fell in love with this land. It was magical.

It had been almost two hours since leaving Santa Fe, and I knew I was getting close to the Ghost Ranch turn off. The road was isolated, with very few cars passing in either direction. It felt like I was driving into the heart of New Mexico. Ahead, off to my right, I saw an opening and a big wooden gateway. As I slowed down, I saw in big letters "Ghost Ranch" with a smaller sign beneath reading "Welcome."

At last, I had arrived. I turned off the main road, through the gate onto a well-traveled dirt road, and slowly followed it up a small hill. At the top stood an old log cabin, and I pulled over to fully absorb the scene. The setting with the cabin, the amazing blue sky, the white clouds, and the majestic mountains in the background had a physical effect on me. Honestly, I felt it in my body and soul, deeply. I knew I was standing on scared ground, and I hadn't driven more than a quarter mile. I couldn't wait to see what was next.

I jumped back in the car, my senses heightened, my adrenaline starting to pump, and drove further. With each turn it was more beautiful, more isolated, and my anticipation grew.

Suddenly, a sign appeared giving directions to different locations on the Ranch. I followed the ones towards the Welcome Center, hardly able to maintain my excitement. I had arrived; I was here. After 10 years of waiting and dreaming, I was here. This was really happening!

There were several cars at the Welcome Center and I found a spot to park. I got out and was suddenly overcome by the heat; it was so hot! I hadn't expected such heat. As I stood there adjusting, I looked around me. I could see the place was much bigger than I expected. As I took in the view I saw buildings of every type in many directions, all built in harmony with the land. And the land was glorious. Each way I looked it seemed picture perfect, more than that, indescribable. The Ranch was surrounded by mountains on three sides and a beautiful panoramic open view of Pedernal

Mountain off in the distance towards the west. The color a rainbow range, from earthy browns and golds, light and dark purple and deep shades of blue, to a variety of greens and everything in between! All intensified by the brilliant blue sky. It was hard to pull myself away to go inside to check in.

Inside the Welcome Center people were milling around. It was rustic, what I had expected, but much less modern. I waited in line near the counter. There must be several retreats starting today; several people were in front of me. I was looking around at them, wondering if any of these women were going to be part of my retreat. I was feeling excited and apprehensive. I also had a little stirring of anxiety. I was always nervous in new situations, and very self-conscious. Finally, it was my turn at the counter. I told the woman my name and the group I was with. She turned behind her on another counter and sifted through some papers. Finding mine, she handed me a map and a couple sheets of paper and told me I would be staying at Staffhouse, Room 17.

"Enjoy your stay," she said.

I left the counter and took a quick tour of the rest of the building. There was a small gift shop/market, a coffee shop, and what looked like meeting rooms. I was wondering if this was where our group would be meeting. The place was filled with people who looked like they knew what they were doing; I totally felt like a newbie. I went back outside and stood for a minute on the patio looking at the map. This place was big; the map showed lots of buildings and even areas for camping. I oriented myself with the map, and I could see that the Staffhouse was directly across a very large meadow from where I stood at the Welcome Center. The map showed a dirt road that circled the meadow. Heading back towards my car, it dawned on me that I didn't get a key. I turned around, went back inside, and waited in line at the counter again.

"Hi," I said to the woman at the counter. "I just realized I didn't get a room key."

"Oh, we don't use keys here. The rooms don't lock," she explained with a smile. "Just find your room; your name should be on the door."

I nodded and walked back outside. That was weird. It felt a bit uncomfortable, but I was going with it. After all, this place had been around for decades; they knew what they were doing. It was out in the middle of nowhere; it was safe.

It was a short drive to the Staffhouse, and I was anxious to see the room. I had requested and paid extra for a private room. I knew I would be processing lots of stuff and didn't want to have to deal with another person. I was thinking how glad I was I had made that decision. I parked the car. The Staffhouse was two long, narrow, brick buildings in a soft "V" shape. Each building had a row of rooms. A screened common area and restrooms were between the buildings.

Room 17 was in the second building near the end. On the outside was a plastic sign holder, and inside it a card that read "Wild Heart Cindy Eubanks." It was right next to a wooden screen door. I opened the door and looked in. The room was a square box with one window and the screen door, two metal twin beds covered by Native American looking wool blankets, and a pillow. There was a small wooden desk, a fan, and two small end tables with reading lights. It was stark. And it was sweltering! New Mexico was having a freak heat wave, and the little room felt like an oven.

I quickly pulled back the curtains and opened the window, then turned on the fan.

Standing there looking around, I wasn't sure what to think. First, I couldn't imagine two people sharing this space, and again was so happy I had paid to have my own room. I knew that it was going to be rustic and simple, but that was an understatement. No room keys, just a simple screen door, a window, and no AC, of course. The brick walls reminded me of my childhood home. I was beginning to freak out a bit. What was going on with me? What had I gotten myself into?

I came here for an adventure, and this was part of it. I needed to change my attitude, and quick! I decided to check out the bathrooms. The closest one was just a few doors down at the end of the walk. It was stark as well, with two toilets, two sinks, and two showers, but looked clean and manageable. I was the only one around, and I knew it would be different when the rooms were filled and felt more alive. I went to my car and began unloading my stuff. It took several trips. Thankfully I had brought a big fan, and I plugged it in and started settling in.

First, I removed the bedding from the bed closest to the window and remade it with things I had brought, sheets, my favorite comforter and two of my best pillows. Sleeping was important to me and I wanted to be comfy. I set up my suitcase on the other bed, hung up clothes, and set up the desk with my art and writing supplies. Before long it was feeling homier. It was still crazy hot, but I could deal with that - I hoped. As I looked around, I thought to myself the simplicity of this adds to the experience and helps set it apart from real life. Yes, that was it. I would remember this and my adjustment. I figured in a couple of days I would either love the simplicity and solitude or I would be going crazy. One way or another, time would tell.

The idea of not having a key was still hard to deal with. I realized my fear was part of being connected with the outside "real" world and I had to let go, yet it was still feeling very real to me. I sat down on my bed, put my feet up, and got out my laptop and wrote for a while. I realized this was a new world, one where I only thought about myself. The responsibilities and obligations that held me captive back in my real life didn't exist here. I was free, unplugged, and had nothing to worry about. No outside communication, just self-exploration. This is what I had been longing for, time for just me. Time to deal with this new wakening to my throat chakra and all the issues that represented. Allowing myself to fully participate in this unknown experience called Painting from the Wild Heart and letting it unfold without resistance. Scary, but exciting. I closed my laptop and decided to go explore. The unease about the open room still nagging me, I hid my laptop and purse, and headed off to see more of the Ghost Ranch.

Dinner was at 5:30 pm and our first gathering (the "Opening Circle") was at 7 pm at the Pinon Room. I got out my map, located both the cafeteria and the Pinon Room, and took off. It was easy to find the cafeteria, it was in the center of everything and pretty close to the Staffhouse, which I was happy about. Dirt roads and paths led to it from every direction. It was a long building with a full front porch that faced west with an amazing panoramic view. The inside was enormous; there must have been enough room to seat two hundred to three hundred people. I was surprised; I hadn't expected the Ghost Ranch to accommodate so many people. It took me back a bit, imagining an intimate retreat in the place where Georgia O'Keeffe called home. This was not that at all. It reminded me of summer camp. The room was empty, but I could imagine it filled with the hustle and bustle of campers talking, laughing, and sharing their adventures. I found the back door and headed towards the Pinon Room.

Checking my map, I followed a dirt road onto a dirt path. There was a sign for the Pinon Room and just beyond I saw the building. It looked a little worn down; it had large covered patios, was "L" shaped, and had all the markings of a preschool or elementary school. It had been well used and loved. From the rear, it faced the range of mountains and hills that surrounded the Ranch towards the east. My mouth nearly fell open at the sight. Again, the brilliant blue sky and white clouds as the backdrop to these spectacular hills. The colors ran horizontally, like the ones I'd seen on the road in, but these hills were close, less than a quarter mile. The peaks and edges were shaped in unique formations, almost prehistoric. At the base were a variety of low growing shrubs and tall trees. The colors were magnificent. Just a few yards away was an open corral, and there were several donkeys wandering around. I stood there, taking some long deep breaths, taking it all in. This is where I was going to be painting for the next six days. It was better than I had ever imagined!

OPENING CIRCLE

"It's okay to be scared. Being scared means you're going to do something really, really brave." - Mandy Hale

Once I felt oriented I headed back to the room and thought I would prepare myself for dinner, whatever that meant. Thankfully people had started moving into the rooms, and I noticed that two women were carrying suitcases into the room next door. We introduced ourselves. They were here for the same retreat, and I was very pleased. They both were open and friendly, and I connected with them right away. It felt good knowing they were right next door. They got settled in, and together we headed for the cafeteria a little before 5:30. We were all anxious to see what it was all about, and glad to be together to face this new experience.

We figured it all out, got our food, and found our table. We were told that we would sit together at the same table every day; this one was assigned to us. Within a few minutes, the table was filling up with new faces. Also, the room was beginning to fill up too; lots of other groups were here for various events. As our table grew, the noise level also grew higher. People were talking about their rooms, the road here, the Ghost Ranch, and how they found their way. It was very exciting to be together. I looked around at the group of women, and I knew this was going to be good. This was a very interesting group.

Unfortunately, that old feeling of awkwardness came over me, a cross between fear and self-consciousness, and I was fighting it like mad. When I spoke, I could feel the shakiness in my throat and the jitters in my chest. Why did I feel like the outsider in every situation? I so wanted this to be different. I had promised myself that I would be open, honest, and vulnerable while I was here. But, it was difficult.

Just then Chris Zydel, our leader, walked in and thankfully my focus shifted. She started hugging people and meeting each of us. I could immediately sense her authenticity. She seemed bigger than life in some ways, yet her down-to-earthiness and open heart filled the space around our table. Her hair was stark white and shoulder length. She was wrapped in a beautiful scarf covering a t-shirt and blue jeans, but what really stood out was her amazing turquoise jewelry. She looked so earthy and goddess-like. I suddenly felt that it was all going to be okay and this was a safe place to be myself. When she came to me, she smiled a big warm smile, hugged me, and told me how happy she was I was here. I could feel my entire body relax and a new sense of ease flooded through me. There was something special about this woman, and I knew at that moment I was in for something very extraordinary. After she made the rounds and welcomed each of us, she sat and joined us for dinner. The rest of the meal was a madhouse of laughter and voices filled with excitement and anticipation. It felt like the retreat had officially begun. As we got up to leave, Chris reminded us to be at the Pinon Room at 7 pm sharp for Opening Circle.

* * *

When I walked into the room, I tried to take it all in without gawking. Around the edges of the room giant pieces of cardboard had been taped to the walls in various spots. Against one wall was a huge stone fireplace with a big hearth. The hearth was filled with candles, stones, rattles, sage, and divinity cards; all kinds of cool and interesting stuff. Chairs were arranged in a circle in the center of the room. There were tables along the front wall filled with every color of paint you could imagine, another one held brushes and big sheets of paper. The candles created an inviting glow, and the room smelled of burned sage. I breathed it in deeply, immediately connecting with that earthy smell and feeling more relaxed and centered. This is it, the beginning of the process.

We all settled in. Chris introduced herself and began to tell us about the process for the next few days. It was interesting and exciting, finally getting a little understanding of what was ahead. It still seemed a bit foreign, but I had a better sense of what to expect. She then took a cloth bag off the hearth and held it in her lap.

"I am going to pass this bag around the circle, and I want each of you to reach in and take an object and hold it in your hand. Don't look at it; just close it in your hand," she instructed.

She then passed the bag to her left, crossed her legs, and sat with a peaceful smile on her face. The first person reached in, and pulled out something small that she closed her hand around. This continued around the room. When I got the bag, I was surprised at its weight. I reached in and felt around; the objects felt slick, and cool, and nearly all of them felt the same. Some part of me wanted to pick the "right" one, whatever that could mean. I let that thought go and just decided to let my intuition do the choosing. I suddenly felt my hand wrap around one; I pulled it out, and passed the bag on.

Once the bag had reached Chris again, she said, "Now it's time to introduce ourselves. You can say as little or as much as you like. Tell us your name, why you came, or whatever you want to share. Then, I want you to open your hand and see what you have chosen from the bag."

Someone bravely went first and that was it; it had begun. We were starting the process of connecting and creating the sacred space, of being a group, and becoming known. I loved this part! Yet, there was still a part of me that was nervous, afraid, and a bit insecure. I paid close attention to each person as they told their story. I was judging myself against them and their stories, then criticizing myself for doing it. My mind was racing around trying to figure out what I would say when it was my turn. Then my mind would judge them, and try to use that to make myself feel better, more experienced, less inferior. I may have sat there looking calm on the outside, but internally I was going crazy. I was questioning my own sanity and wondering why in the world my mind was going off in these crazy directions. Why all the judgment? That feeling of anxiety was setting in, and I immediately went to being fat. I felt too fat to be sitting in the chair; I was suddenly aware of how much of the chair I took up and looked around at other people who had room on the chair, their butts not taking up the entire thing like mine. My pants began to feel tighter, the skin feeling stretched. I was crazy, losing my mind. I fought to bring my attention back to the circle. What was wrong with me? The sane, rational, evolved me seemed to have left the room. The amazing thing was that there was a part of me still listening to the introductions and taking it in; it was like I was split in two. I had to pull myself together, because it would be my turn very soon.

My hand was being held in a fist so tight I had nearly forgotten the object in my hand. But each time someone told their story and then opened their hand to discover what they had drawn from the bag, I was reminded it was there. Each of them was surprised at how connected and relevant the object was to their story. It was finally my turn, and I took a breath, trying to calm myself. My voice was a bit shaky when I started out, but then something sort of swept over me and I was able to talk. I told them where I was from, about how long I had wanted to come, moving to the desert to care for my aging parents, my original reason for coming (to figure out why I keep sabotaging myself), the news about my tumor and how things shifted, and now I wanted to explore healing my throat.

God, I seemed to have made perfect sense. How could I be so crazy on the inside and then behave so seemingly normal on the outside? I was so relieved. I then opened my hand. There in my palm was some type of metal disc with a beautiful relief peacock sitting on a branch. It surprised me; somehow, I never expected a bird. I was thinking a goddess would have been good. Other people picked them. But, a peacock?

I read what it said on the back, "Protection surrounds you in this time of resurrection and rebirth."

I shrugged subtly, not sure what to think, the meaning not resonating. I turned to the person next to me, to signal I was done. She started to tell her story. I quietly took a big sigh of relief and felt the anxiety begin to recede.

As I listened, I sat there looking at the peacock, rubbing my thumb across the raised metal, considering what this might mean. I wasn't sure. But I was a big believer in things having meaning, and I knew I picked this for a reason.

After the opening circle, Chris explained more about the painting process and told us we could stay and pick a spot and get our easels ready, or we could do it in the morning. I decided to claim my spot, and so did many others. I went immediately to the back covered patio, the spot I had seen earlier, the one that overlooked the donkey corral and the beautiful mountains. Painting outside seemed like the right choice. Chris had two assistants, and they helped us set up our stations. It didn't take long. We were ready to start painting first thing in the morning.

We all headed back towards our rooms. It was so dark outside; you could hardly see your hand in front of your face. One of the items we were told to bring on the info sheet we received weeks before the retreat, was a flashlight. I had brought three, but they were all back in the room. It never dawned on me to bring one tonight. (A mistake I wouldn't make in the future!) A group of us, who all were staying in the same area of the Ranch, used our cell phones to light the way. They may not work for making calls, but that night they were great flashlights! It is amazing how dark it can get in the middle of nowhere in New Mexico. It was kind of cool and kind of frightening. Just before we left, Chris had reminded us that there were snakes and other creatures around the Ghost Ranch, to keep an eye out, and to be careful. That info was in the forefront of my mind.

Once back at the Staffhouse, we said goodbye at our front doors. I think all of us were exhausted from the day. When I opened my screen door, the room felt like an oven. Even though I had left the fans on, all they did was swirl around hot air. One thing I was not good with was heat, especially trying to sleep. As I closed the screen door, I noticed there was no lock or latch. It had a hook latch, but one part was missing. The screen door didn't even close all the way; there was a two to three-inch gap at the bottom.

My next thought was, "just enough room for a snake to crawl through."

Yikes! There was a regular solid door, but how could I close it when the temperature was so hot? I would be miserable. A bit of panic ran through me. I crossed the room and checked the window. When I pulled back the curtain, I saw that the screen had been tweaked out of shape and there was another gaping hole there. Fortunately, I was able to bend it back with my hands and close the gap. So now the screen was fitting normally again. But this window looked out the back of the building, and all I saw was dark and the branches of some bushes in the distance.

Creepy, was the first thought that came to my mind. Serial killer creepy. Jason creepy. Friday the 13th creepy.

Oh my God! Get a grip, I told myself. What was I doing? I gave myself a mental slap across the face. I was at the Ghost Ranch for goodness sake - an amazing, peaceful, tranquil place where they didn't even need locks on the doors. It was a spiritual center. What was going on with me? All my fears and anxiety issues were being triggered. Quickly I decided to forget all that, and get ready for bed.

I gathered my things and ventured towards the bathroom. My overactive imagination still messing with me, I checked both bathroom stalls and behind the shower curtains. I took care of business and got the heck out of there.

Back in my room, I brought my laptop out from its hiding place, got into bed, propped myself up, and began to write. I wanted to journal my thoughts as I progressed through this journey and get as much as I could from the experience.

9:30 pm

Don't know what to report. I am trying to be open and be honest and do things different than I normally do. Part of me can't be held back. But other parts of me want to be expressed. I think the hardest thing for me to do this week is to not try to help other people, not judge other people, not isolate myself, and stay out of my head. I LOVE Chris - she is awesome. I trust her and get a true sense of her authenticity - it feels good - she has really good energy. I know this is going to be transforming.

What I wasn't prepared for is the roughing it part. I am feeling vulnerable and scared. Scared of the dark, of the broken screen, and not having a lock on the door. I am hot, and the bed doesn't seem that comfortable. She warned us about snakes and rodents and cliffs that may collapse. I am having a lot of buttons pushed. Fear is really coming up - and it may be because it is all so unfamiliar and I feel exposed. Glad my fellow wild hearts are next door.

Speaking of the people - it is an interesting mix. I feel myself reacting to a couple of them - having my buttons pushed. I am aware of it and hope to see what it is all about. Mostly it triggers my insecurities or parts of myself I don't like - my shadow. We'll see what unfolds.

The other thing that happened tonight is a moment or two of owning who I am, what I have experienced, and recognizing my gifts. I have a bounty of skills, assets, and abilities, and I never really own them in a powerful way. I discount, deflect, or downplay - feeling that I'm too fucked up to be powerful, wise, and experienced. That's bullshit! Maybe part of the week is owning that and not having it be about my ego. When I listened to people tell their stories tonight it was awesome - I love the group process. But, while I was listening, I was also thinking about my life and what I have done that has brought me here and lots of memories came up. I have done so many things and excelled at them. So many creative and spiritual experiences. I've got it - I'm whole and gifted and have so much to offer. What is standing in my way of owning it? Christ, I'd like to know. Okay, seriously, you do know. It is all being revealed - that's what this throat chakra issue is about - it's the full circle of coming home to California and dealing with my mom, my brother, the desert, all of it. Recognizing that taking care of people - needy people has never allowed me to step into my own. I am stuck as a little girl trying to save herself by being outwardly focused for survival and for approval. Never learning to ask for what I need, never knowing how to set boundaries, never learning to stand up for myself and not take shit from people. I was born taking shit from people. I was outwardly focused - my mom was needy and self-centered, she constantly was worried about what other people would think of us - she is shallow and superficial and been ruled by her looks her whole life, yet beneath all that, a complete lack of self-worth. I turned to food for solace and self-nurturing, but learned from my mother that I had to hate my body and eating was bad. All my life I put myself and my best interests aside and did what was best for other people.

Yes, I clearly see why my throat is messed up. But, what I am hoping to do this week is find the way out - a new way of being. Owning the all-powerful qualities I possess and learning to walk in the world as the woman I know I am. And that means from the people I associate with, the way I earn money, to the clothes and jewelry I wear. How I treat my body, how I nurture my spirit, how I make decisions. How I face my fears and choose the life I want to live. It is about stepping up in my own life, and letting that little girl who has been in charge for so long take a break, step back, and let me be a WOMAN - a full grown woman. And that includes being feminine and masculine - and having it be in balance.

The thing that has been getting in my way is a learned behavior - created for the benefit of my family; it was the role I was assigned. And I have continued to act it out for the last 50+ years. This week I want to dismantle that and embrace something new. Something new that doesn't include self-sacrifice and the belief that I am fucked up and need to be fixed. I want to be the truth of who I am - own all my gifts and set a new direction for my life. Step out from behind the curtain of distractions - like being fat and obsessed, the crazy self-consciousness, taking care of others to my own determent, sabotaging myself at every turn. I am feeling so uncomfortable in this fat suit that it is making me crazy! It's time to let it go and step into my wholeness - I don't have to figure that all out right now; I just have to get out of the place I have been revolving around for most of my life, and move in a new direction.

Well, that is a lot to put on this week, but I think it is possible. I know that I am ripe and ready to burst open into a new incarnation of myself. I feel it! Tonight I got a peacock talisman that reads, "Protection surrounds you in this time of resurrection and rebirth." That's it - that's what is going to happen here. And the fears of going back into my life as this new person can be released - for I will be protected. This is a powerful time of connection with my true self and her rebirth from the false beliefs. So exciting!

I closed my laptop, and sat there for a minute thinking about what I had just written. It was a lot to expect from a week. I hope I wasn't setting my sights too high. My mind swirled with thoughts, and suddenly I just felt thoroughly exhausted. I put the laptop on the side table, wiggled around to make myself comfortable in the small bed, adjusted the pillows, and turned off the reading light.

As soon as the light went out, my mind went to the unlocked screen door and the gap. A breeze from the fan moved the window curtain and my mind raced to the scene of creepiness I viewed earlier. A small shot of adrenaline rushed through my body, my eyes popped open, and I just lay there. Wide awake.

Circle, Circles, Circles

"When I go to New Mexico that was mine. As soon as I saw it that was my country. I'd never seen anything like it before, but it fitted to me exactly. It's something that's in the air - it's different. The sky is different; the wind is different. I shouldn't say too much about it because other people will be interested, and I don't want them interested." - Georgia O'Keeffe

It seemed like I had been awake most of the night. The light from the porch shining in my eyes, the heat, the unfamiliar bed, and, of course, the gap in the unlocked screen door. But, somehow, I must have fallen asleep, because now I was waking up from what felt like a sound sleep. As I looked out the screen door, I saw the sky had begun to light up; it was dawn. Sunrise was coming. I got out of bed, grabbed my stuff to take a shower, and headed for the bathroom.

It didn't take me long to get ready and soon I was out walking the land, exploring the Ghost Ranch. It was warm, quiet, and still. The air held its own beauty, so clean and fresh. The views in every direction were beautiful, spectacular. It felt like I was being healed just breathing it all in. It was a whole-body experience, one that is hard to explain. I knew in my heart that I had been called to this land for decades and here I was soaking it in. It felt sacred. My heart grew with every breath I took, and my consciousness expanded. There was a connection growing, way beyond the earth, and I responded to it deeply. I had had this feeling before, on rare, wonderful occasions, and it was always profound, soulful, and spiritual. This morning I was waking up.

I wish I could adequately describe the feeling that came over me just being there. Standing on that land, breathing in the sacredness, and experiencing the oneness. It may sound crazy, but I knew it would be this way. It was sort of an out-of-body feeling, a bit floaty, a bit tingly, a bit like my energy was expanding around my body and connecting with everything in sight and beyond. It was the feeling of connection that begins to take on a new reality. Lines between being human and being spiritual blend together into one, and the area of my heart seems to be at the center of it, radiating and connecting with some essence of unconditional love to the hundredth power. This isn't some hallucination; I am really experiencing it. Tears well up in my eyes, I am overcome with a sense of peace that I have only felt a few brief times in my life, and I am loving it. It is an altered state, but one I want to hold on to! It was clear to me that I had not created this experience; it was being created for me. The more I connected with the beauty of this land, the more connected I felt, the more my heart glowed outwardly, the more acceptance and love I felt. It was spectacular.

I don't know how long I had been standing there; the concept of time seemed to have vanished. But slowly, the feeling began to fade and I became more conscious of my own presence. I kept taking long deep breaths as I reconnected to my physical body, feeling the ground beneath my feet. My mind beginning to process what had just happened, yet allowing myself to feel the deep sense of connection and calm that continued to radiate through me. What a contrast from the scared, crazy, anxious person I was the night before. She had vanished.

I felt happy, joyful, and peaceful. It felt like I had been touched by God. My feet started to move and I began walking, lost in the afterglow of the powerful feeling I just experienced. Something was going on, I wasn't sure what it was, but I recognized it. And it was good. There was magic in this land.

* * *

After breakfast, we all gathered at the Pinon Room. Chris' assistants had smudged the room, the fragrant smell of sage hanging in the air. Just the smell created a mood, and the space seemed more sacred. Everyone was smiling, and there was a sense of excitement in the air. We had name badges that hung around our necks, which helped a lot. This first day was going to be about getting to know each other, I hoped.

Chris came in, welcomed us, and announced that we were going to start the day with movement.

"It's time to get out of your heads and get in touch with your bodies," she announced, then touched the top of a speaker on the hearth. Music started to play.

I knew there was going to be movement, it was the part I was dreading, but knew I needed it. I reminded myself that I had come here to give it my all, so I pushed my fear and self-consciousness away, closed my eyes, and followed instructions. Chris took us through a series of movements, guiding us gently. It wasn't long until I felt the music in my body and let myself just move. It was fun. There were a few people who had been at other Painting from the Wild Heart retreats and they were really getting into it, moving freely, making interesting noises, and doing some radical free flow movements.

At first it was a bit intimidating, but as it progressed I realized it was about freedom. They were leading the way, giving us all permission to express ourselves however it felt natural. I moved outside, because I wanted to be closer to the earth and the sky. I swayed, twirled, and moved my arms and body without regard to anyone watching. I felt free. I let go of the self-consciousness, my size, my awkwardness, and just allowed the music to embrace me.

When the music ended, we all found chairs and formed a circle again. This was our time of sharing. Each person checked in and shared what they were feeling, experiencing, or anything that had come up for them. I did my best to keep focused on each person and their words, but my mind was always jumping ahead. I felt a pull towards those who had sadness come up; I wanted to help them. I had envy for those who shared their successes and judged myself, or became defensive and thought of all the things I have done or that I could do. There were people who didn't know what to share and their vulnerability touched me; I wanted some of that. Then, there were the ones who pushed my buttons. Oh, those were the ones I really paid attention to, knowing that I had found a vein of gold. Here is where my lessons were. I knew it, but I also reacted to them in the way I had before in these same situations. My body tightened up, my heart beating a little faster, and my judging self came to full attention. I was off to the races. It was Elizabeth Campbell all over again. Yes, good old Elizabeth. She had been my "friend" for years, but we shared a love/hate relationship. We were both powerful, strong women doing similar but different spiritual/healing work in the community where we lived. We both triggered something in each other that was not attractive. It was a "let me prove how much better I am then you" kind of thing, but in a subtle, friendly way. I felt she was too out there, bigger than life, always tooting her own horn. I took the low-key approach, always afraid to fully embrace my gifts and take her on, but knowing inside that I was superior. It was crazy and insane, not very spiritual or enlightened of us at all. It took me several years to see her as a teacher and I searched for the lessons, but none of what I uncovered seem to heal the issue. We both were stuck in our egos, and it was hard to overcome. This flashback was helping me see things more clearly.

So here I was face-to-face with it again. Different people, same issue. Part of me was filled with gratitude for this opportunity, and part of me (my old egoic self) was ready to judge and compare until the cows came home. Either way, there was big stuff to learn here. When it came my turn to talk, I sat for a moment trying to gather myself and decide which route I was taking. Thoughts were swimming around in my head, and then suddenly I started talking and it was a cross between the open, vulnerable me I wanted to be and the toot my horn facade that I was trying desperately to fight. Thankfully, it was over quickly and the next person started to share. I knew there was much more to be revealed to me.

"Is everybody ready to start painting?" Chris asked after everyone had checked in.

"Let me go over some things before we start," she continued. "First of all, there will be no commenting on other people's paintings or your own. Our painting time will be quiet, no talking, like meditation."

I could tell people were a bit taken aback, as was I. No feedback, no encouragement, no telling stories about what we each saw in the other's painting! That felt weird. I had been involved with teaching art and helping people embrace their creativity for decades. Giving feedback and encouragement, and finding the beauty in any piece of art was what I did well. The idea of not being able to do that suddenly felt unnatural.

A few people had questions about it. Chris calmly reminded us all, that this was an individual process, an intuitive process, and if we were focused on other people than we would lose touch with ourselves. She explained that she would come around to each of us through the day and check in and help us process our paintings. Her calmness and certainly, plus the fact that she'd been doing this for over 14 years, helped ease my jitters. This was starting to feel a bit uncomfortable, and I knew I had to get pushed out of my comfort zone to shake things up. It was clear this painting retreat was not about becoming a better painter or learning to improve techniques. This was about painting at a soul level, listening to the inner voice, something to do in sacred silence, without the critic mind. That's what I came here for. Although I knew it was impossible to completely silence my critic, I understood the concept. I had come here to engulf myself in the experience, and I was willing to do what it took! So I felt scared - good!

Next, she explained that we were not to be in our "heads" when we painted. She suggested we should stand before the table of paints, let ourselves be led to what colors to pick, then go to our canvas and paint whatever came to us. Just let it go. Then she excused us. Let the painting begin! That was it. We were on our own.

We all went in different directions, some getting paint, others paper, others adjusting their painting spots or finding a new one. My place was already picked out. I had covered it with four sheets of drawing paper all taped together on the back, and then taped and pinned to my easel. It was quite large, nearly four feet by six feet. Big and white. I stood in front of it for a few minutes. A giant while canvas. I felt apprehensive, yet excited. The longer I stood there, the more anxious I became. Suddenly, I knew that I just had to go for it. Dive in. Get out of my head and let my gut lead the way.

Quickly, I headed to the big table full of paints and stood there a moment. Of course, blue and green called to me. My go-to colors. I picked white and black just to play with the shades a bit. I went to the brush table and picked out a variety of brushes, to find a few that "felt" right. And then I made my way back outside to my little studio. Two other women shared the space with me, and they had already started painting. I tried not to be distracted by them or their work, but I noticed right away that both of them could draw, and well. The little voice in my head began talking, and I realized it was happening already, comparing, judging, feeling inferior. It sure didn't take long!

I pushed the thoughts from my head and faced my big blank canvas. I chose one of the big brushes, used a tray as a palette, and began with a squirt of blue and a squirt of white. Circles came to my mind, so I went with it. I started painting a big circle of blue, dark at the center and mixing in white as I moved outwards. It felt good to feel the big brush on the paper, freely painting in big circles. Then I made another and another, all different sizes. I changed my paint to green, a nice bright yet mellow green/yellow color, and started making green circles. My mind trying to create uniformity, and my intuitive self fighting it.

After a while, most of the canvas had been covered with circles. However, there was still one, sort of large space left. The empty space was too close to a big blue circle to make it blue, and too close to several smaller green circles to make it green. I stood there looking at it for a few minutes. I pulled up a chair and sat down, and just stared at it. What to do? I was perplexed. My mind was playing tricks on me. The white spot just glared back at me. Pushing my "it has to be perfect" button. Cripes.

I looked over at the other two painters and was shocked at how good theirs were, how meaningful they seemed. I felt stupid. I was just painting dumb circles and I was freaking out, and these two women were obviously painting something deep, mysterious, and very cool. I started thinking that I must push myself and go deeper. If I wanted to have this work, I had to stop painting like I was in elementary school. I looked away, remembering what Chris had told us, don't judge, don't compare. But I hated my painting, and didn't know what to do. Another thing Chris had said was no starting a new painting without talking to her first and letting her know why we were done. Well, I was anything but done, so I knew I had to move forward.

I went back to the paint table and found some pearlescent paint. That seemed like fun. So, I got it in black and white. I used the white to paint small dots around each of the circles, which added a sort of nice look. But that big white spot kept glaring at me. I went back to the paint table again and stood there. And stood there. And stood there. And suddenly, red jumped out at me.

"Yes, that's it! I'll make a red circle!" I said quietly.

I returned to my painting and proceeded to paint a big red circle. The center was mixed with white, so it was light pinkish red radiating out to dark red on the edges. I liked it. I sat down and contemplated the painting.

Just then one of Chris' assistants came around the corner and announced, "Lunch time!"

The relief I felt was palpable.

Lunch was good. I was hungry, and it felt great just to show up and have food available. Slowly everyone made their way to "our" table. It was our second meal together and it was already feeling more comfortable. In the morning circle, I had mentioned I had been writing a book and was stuck, so at lunch someone asked me about it. At first, I wasn't sure what to say. Should I tell the story or not? A big part of me wanted to tell the story, not because I wanted to talk about the book, more because I wanted them to know I hadn't always been fat. Like they would like me better if they knew I had been thin and "normal." This realization was spinning through my head as I began to speak.

"My book is called *Body Belief.* I started writing it in 2007 after I had lost over 170 pounds and kept it off for nearly six years. During those years I had a difficult time accepting being thin; I kept seeing myself as fat. I realized something was wrong. I began to understand that being fat was a belief system that I held deeply, and no matter what I looked like I still felt fat or felt I looked fat. My doctor told me my BMI was perfect, I was healthy, and I didn't need to lose any more weight, just maintain. I remember looking at him like he was crazy. Couldn't he see that I needed to lose at least 20 more pounds?"

They were listening intently.

"Well, it finally registered and I knew this kind of thinking was bad news. I realized that my thoughts had kept creating my reality most of my life. And if I could change my thoughts and beliefs about my weight, then I could create a new reality, one where I didn't struggle with my weight and body image. So I developed a workshop and a workbook, and started teaching my new philosophy."

Everyone seemed interested and asked questions. And I was feeling good about sharing, but still felt the jitters because the rest of the story was the real truth.

"Then something happened. The more I tried to be aware of my thoughts, the worse I felt and I began eating more and more, binging on pie, chocolate, chips, and ice cream. Before long I started gaining weight, and fast. Within a few short months I gained nearly 80 pounds. The shame was monumental. As I was gaining, I started backing away from my workshop and my book, eventually giving it up all together. I basically went into hiding."

People were still listening. I went on to tell how I decided in 2012 to start working on it again and nearly completed the book, when I began to have self doubts. The idea of writing a book on body image and weight loss and still being seriously overweight seemed ridiculous. I felt like a fraud, so I shelved it just a few months before the retreat.

I realized I had been rattling on and on. Suddenly I became very uncomfortable, and realized that I had over talked. A few people at the table were still listening to me; others had started conversations with their neighbors. I ended quickly.

Several women asked me questions, and I gave short, edited responses. My self-consciousness was growing, and my inner critic was screaming at me. What had motivated me to dump that entire story on the table so quickly? I realized that I desperately wanted them to know that I was a normal-sized person under all the extra weight I was carrying. I also wanted them to know that I had something on the ball, that I was a writer, a coach, that I had done things of value.

Then I realized I was being just like my old friend Elizabeth Campbell and the two women here at the ranch who were pushing my buttons. I was sharing too much, trying to prove that I was somebody, and it was all driven by my ego and a deep seated belief that I wasn't good enough. Damn.

I spent the rest of lunch being super attentive to other people and asking lots of questions. When lunch was over, I decided to head to my room for some solitude, journaling, and to regroup.

> 1:09 pm
>
> Painting has been weird, and also judgmental. I am feeling like my art is crap and I am not going deep enough. Other people are doing far deeper work, and I am just being superficial. I want this to be transforming, and I am afraid that I won't get it. What a set up for myself! It's day one. I have to give myself a break.
>
> I told my Body Belief story to a group of people at the lunch table today; someone asked about my book. Why did I tell it? What do I think that will

accomplish? I want them to know that I haven't always been fat. Like they care. The person it bothers the most is me. Maybe that is what I need to paint about; somehow get below the surface of my fixation with my body image. I need to find what is real, feel whole.

I closed my laptop. It was time to go back for the afternoon painting session; I had to face the circles again. I was feeling tired, hot, and sad. But, I knew I had to keep at it. Back at the canvas, I stared at it again. Suddenly I had the urge to paint the background, so I used the black pearlescent. It took a while to fill it all in, and by the time I was done it looked like a bunch of planets in outer space. I added more white dots around the circles. As I was doing this, a feeling came over me and I realized what I was painting. It became so clear. I had a sudden rush of energy. I saw it. I knew exactly what I was doing. I had clarity in a way of never expected.

The big giant red circle was symbolic of my heart, and all the green and blue circles were all my gifts and talents that I had been ignoring, downplaying, or rejecting. They were lost, floating around, disconnected from me and my heart. I knew instinctively what to do next. I grabbed a brush and started working quickly with purpose.

I drew lines from my heart to each of the circles (my gifts). Each unique and separate gift had its own vein, all connected to my heart. I then painted the lines red to represent the flow of blood (energy) to each one. I added white pearlescent dashes to represent movement - the flow of blood. The painting now represented so much more. As this all came together, I began to feel my heart swell, and a sense of healing overcoming me. All these circles (my gifts) had been isolated and neglected. Now through this painting I was owning them, connecting them to my heart, making them part of my energetic system.

It was profound; tears were streaming down my face. It felt like I was gathering my wholeness with each stroke of the brush. How could this be happening? I sat down and looked at the painting. It still just looked like a bunch of circles, now with red squiggly lines attached to the big red circle. But, it was much more than that for me. How had this painting transformed from paint on paper to this enormous feeling of healing that I was experiencing? My breathing was deeper, my shoulders were pushing back, and I could feel my posture change. I was having some internal and external physical reaction to this painting, and the process. I was owning the lost parts of myself that I had been shunning, ignoring, and denying for most of my life. Sitting on the patio, with the stunning New Mexico skyline as a backdrop, painting from my wild heart, I was feeling healed in a way I never experienced before. Something magical was happening to me, and I was loving it!

Now I got it. When Chris told us, "you'll know when you are done" (with a painting), she was right. I knew I was done with this one. It felt complete. It had taught me what I needed to learn. I was ready to move on. It was an exhilarating feeling.

PAST LIFE OR APPARITION?

"Past life memories don't come from your mind, they come from your soul. They lead you to familiar people and places. You don't think them, you feel them." - Anita

The evening program was being presented by one of the assistant leaders, and it was called Seeing with your Heart. Since I had promised myself to participate fully, I was back in the Pinon Room a little before the starting time. The room was set up with a circle of chairs in the center. The lights were off, candles illuminated the room, and the smell of sage was in the air again. In the center of the circle were four candles. I knew these represented the four directions.

Alongside the candles were all kinds of rattles, small drums, and shakers. It wasn't long before all the chairs were filled. Most everyone was here; only a couple of people opted out. Jasmine, the leader, began by opening the circle, lighting the candles for each direction. She explained that she was taking us on a Shamanic Journey. But, first we must begin to raise the energy in the room. We would do this using the instruments, chanting, dancing, and doing whatever we felt moved to do.

I was paying attention with the openness I had promised myself I would have towards the entire experience, but something was beginning to feel weird. At first, I tried to ignore it. I was intrigued by Jasmine, and I was sure this was going to be a great experience. However, something was not feeling right for me. Each person picked a noisemaker or an instrument and the music began. With the rattles and drums, it began to sound like some ritualistic Native ceremony. I had picked a beaded shaker. My eyes were closed, and I was shaking it.

Suddenly, Jasmine began making sounds like coyote hoots. Others joined in with wolf howls and lots of yipping. The volume rose; it was getting louder and louder. Something flooded through me, and I went from feeling uncomfortable to a sense of fight or flight. I kept my eyes closed and kept shaking the shaker, but something was happening to me. Part of me felt angry, and another part of me just wanted to get the hell out of there. I had no idea what was going on, but it was real and powerful. This wasn't the first time I had been in this type of situation. I had participated in drumming and chanting circles dozens of times. This, however, something weird was happening to me.

The discomfort I had was nearly over powering. Honestly, I was shocked by my reaction. It seemed like the dancing, chanting, and drumming was never going to end, but thankfully it did. Hoping that would help, I sat down in my chair. Jasmine started explaining how she would lead us in a journey, and gave instructions to the group. The entire time my mind was focused on how I could leave without bringing a bunch of attention to myself. I didn't really understand the sensations I was feeling, but it was real. I talked to myself, took some deep breaths, and tried to settle down.

Jasmine started to guide the group through the first journey. It was all about finding our power animal. I tried to follow along and visualize the process she explained, but something kept me from connecting. I had this anger building in me that just didn't make sense. I was so uncomfortable and wanted to be any place but here. Some part of me knew that because I was having this type of reaction, there had to be something big I needed to look at, but I was having a hard time even caring.

The first journey ended, and Jasmine asked if anyone would like to share what happened. Someone quickly raised their hand and told the story of coming into contact with their power animal and how beautiful it was, how connected they felt. One by one, people told similar stories with all types of animals showing up, bears, owls, wolfs, elk. I just sat there a bit freaked out by how connected everyone was and how disconnected and detached I was.

Jasmine then took the group through a second journey, this time to find the power animal that connected us to our sacred spiritual selves. She started talking about throwing a red cord down a hole and following the red cord. I tried desperately to follow her voice and had my eyes closed tightly. I tried to imagine following a red cord into the darkness, but it wasn't working. I felt fidgety in my seat, I felt hot, and all I wanted to do was leave. I considered going to the bathroom and then sneaking out the back door. The internal struggle that I was under felt exhausting; all I was trying to do was relax, let go, and follow Jasmine's voice, but it wasn't happening. Again, at the end people shared amazing stories of what they had seen or experienced on their journey. I was flabbergasted that we were in the same room and I was having such an entirely different experience.

Jasmine then did the third journey. This time I told myself I was going to do it, just push through. She started the visualization, and I tried to stay connected. I imagined in my mind a blue heron; yes, a blue heron. I had had an amazing spiritual experience that involved a blue heron when I lived in Ohio, so I was visualizing that. I could see the heron standing on a log in the Cuyahoga River, me sitting on a big rock, and I could hear the water rippling down through the valley.

But suddenly, this voice in my head said, "Bullshit! You can't just make up something you already experienced."

I realized I was doing this so I could have a story to tell at the end, so I could be like everyone else, so I could feel like I was part of what was happening. Sadness fell over me, and I resigned myself to getting through this evening. It couldn't be much longer until I could go back to my room.

The third journey was over and it was time to share. Again, interesting and amazing stories; some people brought to tears by their shamanic journey.

After everyone had told their story, Jasmine looked at me and asked, "Cindy, do you want to share anything?"

I looked at her for a moment, trying to decide whether I should tell the heron story and pretend it happened in the journey or say nothing.

Finally, I said, "No", and just shook my head slightly.

Thankfully, she moved on. She announced that we would have one last, final journey for the night, and it would be the longest. She described what we were going to do. I just sat there, half listening, thinking about what was wrong with me, and why I was having this reaction. I couldn't figure it out, but I knew I had to let go of this anger and fear that had me in its grip. Why was I so pissed off and so uncomfortable?

Jasmine started talking, leading the group into the last journey. The room seemed to get so quiet, not a single sound. The silence affected me, and I connected with it. My eyes were closed and I was breathing deeply, just concentrating on the silence. I had let go of any expectations to try to do the journey; instead I just focused on the silence and being present. I could feel myself begin to calm down. I realized I needed to let go. I'm not sure if it was because I knew this would be over soon or if I had just had a moment of surrender. Either way, it felt better and I was relieved.

Suddenly, I began to feel something odd; it was like a tingling sensation coming over my body. It was a bit like electricity, and the hairs on my arm started to stand up. It startled me, but I kept my eyes closed and just let it happen. The anxiousness, anger, and fight/flight feelings I was experiencing before were completely gone. My focus had moved from my head to my body, and I felt a bit like I was floating. Time suddenly stood still. I felt a sensation like I was moving backwards and up. In my mind I was moving away from the group, and I was looking down at the circle.

My eyes were still closed but I could see this clearly, like a vision. It felt very strange, but I wasn't afraid. I could see all the women sitting in their chairs with their eyes closed and the candles in the center with all the rattles, drums, and shakers. It was all a bit blurry and sort of foggy, but I could see the scene. Just then I began to feel a presence next to me. At first it just felt like energy, something bright and warm.

Soon, I sensed it was a person. It was a young man and he was sort of like a hologram, not fully there, a bit see-through, but very real. I could see he was a young Indian man. He had long hair and was dressed in Native American clothing. Amazingly, I wasn't scared or freaked out; it all seemed normal, and real.

We were standing there next to each other, his arms crossed, looking down on the circle, and he said to me, "Look at all these white women."

I just nodded my head.

"Looking for ritual and spiritual connection and taking ours."

There was a sense of knowing between us. He didn't have to talk, but I could understand his message so deeply and profoundly. Now I understood my discomfort and anger earlier in the evening. Thoughts came into my mind, like his words were being spoken in my head.

"My people have been massacred, the land stolen, why must they take our sacred spirituality? Don't they know?"

It was like he was speaking a great truth to me on a sensory level. It was about the greatest truth, that we are all connected and the essence of our spiritual nature is in us. That each of us can find a way to connect with that; it is part of the soul essence within us.

For a minute, my mind drifted off and remembered a white woman I once knew who had lived on the Lakota Rose Bud Reservation for years. She created her own rituals, unique to her and every situation she faced. She told me ritual comes from inside; it is a natural process evoking connection to the Great Spirit.

She called it, "spirituality by the seat of your pants."

130

It made me smile, remembering all the rituals we had created together. She understood on some level that co-opting Native spiritual traditions wasn't right. As white people we were too conditioned to act within the norms of our culture, yet we yearned for ritual and meaning. So she just made up her own! She had been one of my first great spiritual teachers.

The presence of the hologram was filling the space around me, and it was gentle, loving, and radiated acceptance. He seemed to stand tall, strong, and was filled with conviction. I could feel it on a physical level vibrating through me. He was here to give me this gift of knowing, a message of truth. The power of our innate connection to the source, the Great Spirit, God, exists within us, and ritual is what helps bring us into connection.

I also understood on a deep level that the two of us were connected, somehow, somewhere, some time, some place. We knew each other. Tears began to flow down my face, and I was overcome with a sense of deep love and peace. I let myself be absorbed into it. Knowing that somehow, I would never be the same again.

Jasmine was talking slowly and quietly, and I realized she was calling us back from the journey. I felt myself in my chair, my feet on the ground, tears still rolling down my cheeks. I wiped my face, and slowly opened my eyes. It felt weird, like I had been away, and returned as a stranger to this room. Very odd. It took a moment to adjust and re-connect. Then it dawned on me that this time I had something to share about the journey, but I wasn't sure I wanted to. I listened to others tell their stories. Some of them amazing, beautiful, and transforming.

When I finally spoke, I said, "I'm not sure what happened to me. But I think I had some type of past life experience. Whatever it was, it was good."

And that's all I had to say. I needed to get my head around what had just happened to me! Again!

The circle was closed. We all headed back to our rooms, chatting about the experience. I didn't talk; I didn't know what to say. I thought if I told them what had happened to me, they would think I was a bit crazy. Plus, it felt too intimate and personal; I didn't want to share it with anyone.

Once back in my hot room, I sat on the bed and tried to get my mind around what had happened. That was the weirdest thing I had ever experienced, and it had felt REAL! But I knew it was just my imagination playing out some vision for me. I wanted to be part of the experience, so my mind created something so I could feel included. I kind of laughed. Yes, that must be it. Then I thought, or could it really have been some past life thing? A little spark of energy ran through my body. I was confused, and a little freaked out. Another change of focus was in order, maybe a shower. I grabbed my stuff, and headed to the bathroom.

The shower helped. Once back in my room, I locked the screen door. Earlier in the day, I had found an empty room and unscrewed the eyehook from that door and put it on mine. So now the basic hook and eye lock on my door worked again. It felt good to feel safer and not so worried about snakes slithering in while I slept! I grabbed my laptop, got into bed, and journaled about the day. Processing all my thoughts helped, and I was feeling more relaxed. The room was still hot; the fans blowing air helped, but sleep was far from my mind. The events of the evening were still running through my head, and I wasn't sure what to make of the whole thing.

I put my laptop away, turned off the light and lay there, staring at the ceiling, wondering if what I had experienced had been real. And if it was real, what did it mean? And if it wasn't real, why had I imagined something so visceral? Plus, I didn't feel like I wanted to tell anyone, because somehow it would seem like judgment about their process, and that wasn't at all what I felt. It was just for me, some lesson, some way of helping me understand that whatever I need is inside of me, the answers are within, that I must find my own path to the divine. Or the awareness of the deep thread of spirit that runs through all people, no matter their culture, rituals, or customs.

My mind was spinning. It had certainly been an interesting first day.

Truth, Grace, and a Healing Map

*"I do not at all understand the mystery of grace - only that it
meets us where we are but does not leave us
where it found us." - Anne Lamott*

The light from the porch shined in my eyes most of the night and kept me awake. I had gotten up and closed the solid door sometime in the middle of the night, but then the heat was too much and I got up and opened it again. It had not been a good night. Tossing and turning, building a pillow blockade from the light, then knocking it down. I felt worn out. It was still warm. Nights at the ranch haven't been too good for me.

I looked outside and saw the beautiful morning, and my attitude improved. It was still early and seemed so quiet, so I got up, dressed, and took a walk. The memories from the journey the night before were rolling around in my mind, and I still wasn't sure what to make of it. The glorious morning helped clear my head. Within minutes I was feeling refreshed, renewed, and filled with energy from the land, sky, and clear air. This place was like living in an art show. Every minute it changed from the light, the shadows, the clouds moving through the sky, the sun raising, peeking out behind a mountain, or light rays glistening through the trees. It was powerful, and immediately livened my spirits.

After a while I realized it must be getting close to breakfast, so I headed for the cafeteria, ready for some morning coffee. I took big, long, cleansing breaths as I made my way. I was looking forward to the day ahead, uncertain of what would come along next!

After breakfast, I found Chris. I said if she had some free time, I would like to talk to her about something.

She said, "How about now?"

"That would be great," I answered.

We found a private table, and sat down.

"There are a couple of people here who are really pushing my buttons, and I am wondering if that is something I can talk with you about?" I asked.

"Absolutely!" she said with that loving, accepting way she has about her. "Tell me about it."

"Well, like I said, there are a couple of people, one in particular, that are bringing some old feelings out in me. Since I hardly know them, I get that it is something about me. I want to deal with it, but I'm not sure how."

She asked me a few questions, and wanted to know who it was. I told her, and described the behavior that triggered me. I told her about my old "frenemy" Elizabeth Campbell, and how the reaction was exactly the same. It was all about them self-aggrandizing and telling stories of what they have done, people they know, etc., etc. It just seemed like they were trying too hard to feel important or valued, and it came off making me feel weird just listening to them. Something about it hit too close to home. I really didn't feel I was like that, but some part of it was pushing my buttons. I thought of Debbie Ford and her books on the Shadow Self, and I knew there was power attached to all this. I really wanted to uncover it, and heal it for good!

Then she asked me, "What would you like to say to them?"

I thought for a quick second, and said, "You are enough."

"Ah, so you have compassion for them," Chris nodded her head.

"Oh yes, some part of me sees that it is all about feeling good enough and self-worth issues. I want to tell them, 'You are enough exactly as you are' and I want to tell myself that too!" I responded, suddenly overcome with sadness; I felt like I wanted to cry.

This short interaction with Chris suddenly began to open up this issue, and things began to make sense.

"I think I'm understanding. There is a part of me that wishes I could stand up and own my talents and gifts, and I don't know how to do that appropriately, so I downplay myself, or at least I feel I do. Then when I see people like them, my button pushers, they are doing it in a way that makes me feel uncomfortable, like they are bragging. And that feels bad too. It's like two ends of the spectrum. I can't toot my own horn and they over toot theirs. Or at least that is what I am hearing them do. No one seems to be bothered by it but me."

I realized that it was so easy for me to downplay my gifts, or get embarrassed telling about things I am good at, but they seemed so at ease with it. In my eyes, I didn't want to be like them, but I didn't want to be like me either. There had to be some place in the middle that felt comfortable and right - just enough.

"Is there someone in your life who has modeled the behavior you are looking for?" Chris asked me.

I had never thought of that before. I took a few minutes and thought about it. I couldn't think of anyone. Actually, Chris seemed like a perfect model, but I had only known her a couple of days.

"I can't think of anyone right now," I answered.

"Why don't you give it some thought, maybe write about it, and see if you can come up with a description of how that person would be. Who you would want to be," she suggested.

That was a great idea. I thanked her, and she hugged me. Before she left, she asked me if I would be willing to talk about this at the opening circle this morning, leaving out names, of course. I thought for a minute, and told her I would consider it. She smiled, I smiled, and we both set off to start our day.

That morning at the circle I did talk about it, and it felt good to express such honesty. It occurred to me that my circle painting the day before was part of that process. Recognizing that I must own my gifts and accept them without fear. It felt weird, but I knew I was on to something.

Embracing Grace

Looking back on all this, I can see how this day clearly had a theme and a message for me. Earlier, Chris had led us in the movement part of the day. She directed us to move in "themed" ways - happy, excited, etc. The one that hit me was when she asked us to move with "grace." It was hard for me to connect, to move in a graceful way. Never had I considered myself graceful; I had always felt self-conscious and awkward. I closed my eyes as I moved and tried to pull the feeling of grace from somewhere inside me, but I couldn't.

Then suddenly, I thought of my daughter-in-law, Kelly. Kelly was a ballerina, and had been since she was a young girl. I thought of her, and how she just radiated a sense of grace, from the way she walked, the way she held her head, her long neck, her hands and arms; grace just poured from her. It was part of her being every minute of the day. So, I decided to channel her. I connected with the music, just held her essence in my mind and heart, and began to feel like I was in a trance. It was wonderful. Normally I would feel fat, awkward, and shy, but suddenly I felt graceful, light on my feet, and beautiful. It was a tremendous feeling; my heart was opening, and I felt joyous.

As I twirled around the room, with my eyes closed, channeling Kelly's beauty and grace, these words floated into my head, "Accept Your Gifts with Grace!"

The words, the message, just kept repeating itself as I moved.

"Accept Your Gifts with Grace!"

It was a surreal feeling, nearly like an out-of-body experience. I had never felt this elegant and graceful, and hearing those words evoked deep emotion within me. Like Kelly's gift of grace, which was her very essence, I must do the same with mine. It is a gift, a birth gift. Just as she was born to dance, I was born to own my gifts.

A great sense of peace washed over me, and I was filled with emotion yet again. After just a matter of minutes spent in this space, I was beginning to feel healed. I understood that it was time for me to step into the grace of my own being. Until I could fully accept my gifts, I will never be able to be the woman I talked with Chris about being. I was finally getting it.

After the morning movement and circle, we went back to our painting. All the women made their way quietly back to their painting spaces; there was no talking, no laughter, everyone was focused on the process.

I noticed others' paintings. Some of them were giant, filling nearly an entire wall. These were going to become masterpieces of internal flow. But, the big ones scared the hell out of me.

Since I had finished the circle painting the day before, I was ready to start a new one. I decided to go small, and I picked up one two foot by three foot sheet of paper. It felt safe and comfortable. I taped it to my easel and prepared to paint. I sat down and looked at the blank paper for a while. Then I began to feel something. It's funny how the process just starts to take over.

Suddenly, I envisioned a body, but not the whole body, just the mouth, neck, and torso. I drew an outline. The throat and neck section was long, unrealistically long, and I knew this was going to be about my parathyroid tumor. My brush seemed to be working on its own and I was drawing my thyroid and parathyroid. (A few weeks earlier I would have had no idea how to paint them, but after doing so much research since I was diagnosed, it was easy.) Then I drew the tumor. I painted it gold, like a jewel.

Stepping back to look at it, I knew I had to turn the thyroid into a butterfly, and that's what I did next. Again, I stepped back to look at it, then my attention moved to the beautiful blue and white sky in the distance. I turned back to the painting, and recreated that sky and clouds in my painting as the background behind the body. It felt great!

The whole time I was painting, I was thinking about the newly diagnosed tumor, my lifelong thyroid issues, and my 5th chakra. Physically I could feel the tightening of my throat, it being filled with a blockage. I also realized that this tumor was a messenger, and I needed to understand it. Already I knew that it was about so much more; swallowing my feelings, not speaking my truth, withholding my needs, stuffing my desires, and avoiding anger and pain.

An idea floated into my head, and I went to find a pencil. On the upper part of the painting, by the mouth, I wrote, "SMILE, STUFF, INTELLECTUALIZE, DENY."

Then below the neck on the torso, I drew an arrow pointing down and wrote, "Ignored" and "FEAR, TRUTH, VALUE, VOICE, NEEDS, WANTS, DESIRES, ANGER, and PAIN."

On the left side of the torso, I drew a big empty heart.

The look reminded me of an old 1960's concert poster.

I went to the paint table and grabbed a bunch of wild colors. I came back, and started painting the background around the words in a variety of colors.

At the bottom where I had written ANGER in big letters, I painted flames.

140

As I painted, I was overcome with anger that I had lived 58 years and had never allowed myself to fully express myself. I had been holding all this down for decades, and it wanted to bust loose.

Chris had come into the porch area and was making her rounds, talking quietly as one after another of us opened up and processed our paintings with her. She pulled a chair up and sat down next to me. She asked me to tell her about my painting.

I looked at her, and then I looked at my painting.

"It sort of looks like a concert poster from the 1960's," I said.

"I get that," she replied with a smile. "What does it mean to you?"

I wasn't sure, but I started to talk anyway.

"I think I am painting this to try and figure out what is happening with my throat. It's like I have to get it through my head what is happening. I have spent my life stuffing my feelings, doing what I thought others wanted me to do, and being who they wanted me to be. Hell, I realize now that I have even been stuffing my own physical pain!"

"Wow, that's a biggie," she said in the most loving, understanding, comforting way.

"Yes, it is. How can I deny my own physical pain?" I shook my head. "So I am painting this, so I can dig deeper into it and really see what needs to change."

"Seems to me you are painting a map. A map to guide you to healing and wholeness," she responded.

I laughed, with a tear in my eye and a lump in my throat.

"Yes, that's it. It's a map. It's going to show me the way to recover. With each word I paint, I feel like I am going deeper and deeper into understanding the whole thing. It brings me to tears as I'm doing it," I admitted.

"So, you still have juice for this painting?" she asked me, with a coy smile on her face.

Again, I laughed, "I sure do!"

"Well, then, keep at it," she stood up, smiled at me, and carried her chair off to the next painter.

By the end of our afternoon session, I had learned so much from my painting. I had painted a map, one that led me to understand a condition, a lifestyle that ended up manifesting illness in my body - a tumor in my throat. I knew there was more to uncover, but it was also time to take a break.

WISDOM AND THE PEACOCK

"Knowing yourself is the beginning of all wisdom." - Aristotle

After dinner, I headed back to my room. I lay on the bed, thinking about the day - the talk with Chris, the connection with Kelly and "grace," the painting, my map to healing. It was a lot.

I remembered that Chris had asked me to write about what being balanced around my gifts would look like, so I got my laptop out of its hiding place (which seemed stupid by now), piled pillows behind my back, and prepared myself to type.

I sat for a moment thinking about what balance would feel like. If I just accepted my gifts with grace, who would I be? What would that feel like?

Allowing that feeling to fill me from my heart and not my mind, I started typing:

> Calm, peaceful, and even-tempered. Exudes a quality of wisdom and power - but with a foundation of loving-kindness. She is secure in her knowledge and beliefs, and will gently share when the time is right. Self-confident, self-aware, and spiritually connected. She practices sacred selfishness, and knows how to set boundaries with ease. She is strong, and faces fear

head on. She embodies her essence with grace, ease, and charm. Truly authentic in body, mind, and spirit. There is a completeness that feels real and true - from her voice, demeanor, beliefs, and even the way she dresses. Open, self-assured, loving, and aware. Living life is a practice of her deepest knowing.

Yes, that was it. Confident, but not arrogant. Gentle, but not a doormat. Living mindful and aware of herself in a whole, complete way. Not driven by ego, but connected to an inner understanding of her own greatness.

I liked it. It felt complete. I closed the lid of my laptop.

I sat there, my mind reviewing this day, the night before, the whole day before. The process of jumping from one issue to the next. It was mind-boggling. I began to realize that all these issues were related. It all was going to come together and make sense; I could feel it coming. When I thought about this trip, this retreat, I had no idea I would be sitting here having experienced what I had so far. It seemed overwhelming, but I knew it was right. The time had come; I was ready to heal.

Just then, I had the urge to go back to my painting. Yes, it was calling. I put on my shoes, and headed back to the Pinon Room.

For the next two hours, I painted the words on my map. While painting each word, I immersed myself in its meaning. What it meant in general, what it meant to me, and how I had lived this word in my life. Each letter flooded me with memories. I was remembering things I had long forgotten, seeing things in an entirely new light. I was overcome with sadness and pain. I was feeling this process on a level I had never touched before, but now understood. It was clear to me that this tumor was a gift.

After painting for a while, I became worn out from the intensity. I was beginning to lose my "juice." It was time to clean up and go.

I headed back through the main room, the room with the big fireplace. A couple of people were still painting; I walked quietly. As I passed the hearth, I stopped to admire the altar. It looked beautiful, with candles, shells, sage, and all the rattles and instruments from the night before. There were also several decks of divination cards and a couple of animal books, describing the meaning of all types of animals. I thought of the ritual last night and my reaction, and then remembered the peacock I had chosen the night before. I picked up the book, flipped through the pages, and found the one describing peacocks. I read it:

> *"Let yourself stand out and be noticed!"*
>
> *It's time to step forward and stop hiding behind any of the facades that you've developed over the years. Although these personas have been highly adaptive and have helped you along the way—for which you can be grateful—there's more of you to express to the world, and it's ready to emerge. There's a certain safety and comfort to being inconspicuous and always staying in the background, yet in playing it safe in this way others don't have the opportunity to get to know who you really are, and you don't get to experience the richness and textures that are possible by participating more fully in life. By remaining in the background, you not only alienate others, but often end up allowing*

others to choose for you. Doing so can make you feel like a passive victim.

"Oh, yeah," I thought, and continued reading.

Being noticed does have some risks. People may criticize or judge you, particularly if they're used to you not asserting yourself in such a way. Or you may judge yourself, which can be an even harsher sentence. These are the most likely risks, but they're actually very minimal. So, shed any guilt or shame about coming out with who you are. Wear more colorful clothing, sing, dance, and let others know your thoughts, feelings, and opinions. You can do so with grace, dignity, and enthusiasm—you might even enjoy it!

I read it again. I took out my phone, and took a picture of the page. This meaning of the peacock hit me like a slap in the face. This description seemed to encompass all the events of the retreat, all the seemingly separate happenings, and brought them together in wholeness.

This was about me stepping into my own truth, owning my true essence and the gifts, letting go of what other people think, and finally being me - no excuses or fears. This peacock thing was beginning to make more sense. I suddenly realized that I had found my power animal!

I checked the clock, and realized it was nearly time for the next and final event of the day. Several of us were meeting with Chris to process what had been happening for us at the retreat. It was a sign-up situation, and only eight people could attend. She did two of these sessions during the week, and I had signed up for both. I wondered if this was going to be too much since I had had such an eventful day, but that's the reason I wanted to go. I needed to process.

A group of us made our way up the hill to the meeting. It was a short distance from the main ranch. It was a lovely evening, the sun was gently setting, and the view was breathtaking. As walked, we laughed and shared stories, constantly commenting on the beauty that surrounded us, stopping to take pictures. It felt good to be together. None of us knew what to expect, but we were excited.

Chris was waiting for us when we arrived. It was a small cabin with chairs, a couch, and a table. We all made ourselves comfortable.

Chris explained that we would each have 15 minutes to talk, and then if we chose to do so we could get five minutes of feedback from the group.

We got started. The stories were amazing. Everyone was having similar experiences to mine, but with different issues. Many were overlapping.

One woman talked about painting fetuses, and how that surprised her. She then talked about having had four abortions. She was deeply moved; she thought she had worked through that long ago, but now it was coming up in a different way.

That shocked me a bit; I didn't see that coming. It hit me like an arrow in my heart. My mind drifted off as I remembered the three abortions I had in my twenties, ending with having my tubes tied at age 28. Me, the girl who talked all through my childhood and young adulthood about wanting eight kids - four boys and four girls. There was nothing I wanted more than to have a bunch of kids. My heart felt heavy listening to her story, realizing that I too thought I had worked through that issue. I made a mental note to talk to her later about it, in private.

Another woman talked about living in a sexless relationship, but still loving her partner and not knowing what to do. She desperately wanted romance, passion, and intimacy. They were best friends, but unfortunately, he felt more like a brother to her.

Ouch, another hit, bull's-eye. As I listened to this amazing group of women, I felt stronger, braver, and not so different. We were all seeking wholeness, love, and self-acceptance.

My turn came. I felt limp, not sure what to say, not sure I even had the energy to share, but I did. My story felt sad. I don't really remember what I said, but I have a feeling memory. I also recall getting feedback about being honest. It felt strange, since I didn't feel like I was ever really honest with myself. I was always being what I thought other people wanted me to be, and never succeeding.

I was tired. Two nights without good sleep and all this emotional upheaval had caught up with me. I just wanted to go to bed.

My Little Pony Birthday Party

"Laundry is the only thing that should be separated by color." -
Author Unknown

My hopes of a good night's sleep, were just that, hope. The heat, the porch light, the discomfort, and my fears had kept me awake on and off the entire night. I felt completely worn out. Yet again, a part of me was ready to begin a new day. My thoughts kept going back to the talk last night, especially my unfinished business with the abortions and what all that meant. I needed to talk to Erica, the woman who had brought it up last night. Maybe we could process it some together. I decided to talk to her at breakfast, to see if she had some down time today to talk.

As I walked to breakfast, I thought about all the stuff I was working through all at once. I realized how many head games I play with myself, how much I blame myself, how much I stay in the victim mode. My throat, my fear of my own power, my past. I knew I was getting close to stepping in to my own power and out of that victimhood role. The victim is gone, the Goddess will rise! I laughed at that, but what else could I call a powerful, self-confident woman? Just thinking that felt foreign and a tad uncomfortable, but I knew that I had to stand in my strength and own it. How could I be embarrassed or feel silly? Spending my life being a victim and a people pleaser was over. It had to be. I needed to be ready to embrace something new, and that involved owning my POWER. I could see that clearly. It was time. It was coming.

At breakfast, I talked to Erica and we agreed to talk later. I didn't tell her what it was about. I just said I wanted to talk about "something that came up last night." She was open and willing.

I then headed to morning circle for more movement and more connecting with my body. This felt so awkward and uncomfortable at first, but always felt great once I got into it. I knew that getting out of my head and into my body was what I had needed for years. I also knew that this connection was part of the reason so much was being revealed to me and so much was being healed.

The entire process that Chris developed was amazing, and then doing it at this sacred location made it something very special. Every activity led me closer towards being whole. I had left home feeling like I was broken, screwed up, and in need of fixing. But, this morning I felt entirely different. I was starting to really feel what my mind could only comprehend just a few short days ago. It was a feeling of being whole, strong, and enough - just as I was.

Back at the easel, I sat in front of my throat "map" and contemplated what I would do next. Did it still have juice, as Chris would say? I think it did.

I gathered some painting supplies and made a few finishing touches. I again sat and thought about what it all meant. The idea that I ignored physical pain still hit me hard. I had realized yesterday that I had experienced daily headaches for months and never did anything about it. I just ignored it, not even taking a Tylenol or aspirin. When I was diagnosed with the tumor, I found out headaches were one of the side effects. Along with leg aches and joint pain, which I also disregarded, blaming myself, thinking being fat was causing it.

I also remembered my mom always talking about how I never complained about pain. She went on and on about how I would be hurt and never say anything. Somehow it made me feel proud. I had learned to bury my pain, even as a child.

This painting really woke me up. It stood for so much; it explained so much. Each word, FEAR, TRUTH, VALUE, VOICE, NEEDS, WANTS, DESIRES, ANGER opened fully before me as I painted them. Each unfolding new truth I had to face, telling me a story of my life. The words above my neck, SMILE, STUFF, INTELLECTUALIZE, DENY were so true, each one uncovering a method I had chosen to keep my feelings at bay, to ignore myself. Coping mechanisms for protection, or it had seemed that way.

I knew I couldn't look at this issue the same again. It was crystal clear that it was time for me to learn how to love and care for myself, to listen to my own body, and pay attention to its messages. I had to seriously start speaking my own truth, living my authentic life, and owning my talents and bringing them forward. There was much to be healed, and I knew it was happening whether I felt ready or not! I must have sat with my painting for over an hour, just absorbing the message. I got it.

I found Chris, and told her I was finished with my painting. She came over, and we talked about it. I told her all about what I had learned, and how I was feeling. She helped me process even more; it felt so good to finally understand. She gave me a hug and then the go-ahead to start a new painting.

After lunch, I got started. This time I wanted to go big, so I filled my entire space with paper. My new canvas was taller than me and about five feet wide. It was fun preparing it, but soon I was back to the blank canvas stare. This time, a giant white canvas. Well, not giant like some of the women were painting, but big to me. I didn't have a clue what to paint, and I didn't want to think about it too much.

I remembered Chris telling us this morning to just stand at the paint table and let your feelings, your gut pick what colors it wanted to paint. I knew I had to stay out of my head. So that's what I did. I took my palette tray and stood in front of the paint table; I walked back and forth, just letting my "feeling sense" take over and waited. Out of the blue, I started picking up blinding florescent colors - yellow, pink, green blue. My mind started to judge, and I let it go.

Back at the canvas, I started to paint. I made a bright pink line across the top at a sloping angle. Then I started to make random marks in all the space above the line. I switched between colors and made sort of an abstract design effect. It was fun. I felt like a little kid. Of course, there was still judgment going on in my head, comparing my painting to others within my view, and the ones I saw in the big room where the paints were, but I had to let that go. I was going to just paint whatever came, whatever that looked like, without judgment. I felt defiant, just like a kid! Just then I thought, glitter! Yes, that what I need, glitter paint!

I went back into the paint room and looked for glitter paint.

 Chris was standing nearby and I said to her, "My painting is hurting my eyes."

"Why?" she asked.

"Somehow I needed to use florescent colors," I said with a smile.

"Too bright, huh?"

She laughed.

"You better get used to it!" Chris added.

When she said that I knew what she meant. She was talking about my own brightness, letting my brightness shine. It seemed to make perfect sense but yet made me laugh, like it was silly.

Back at the painting, I used the glitter to add sparkle to the already bright glow. It was great fun to add the glitter, but after a while I had run out of space to paint in the top section. It seemed that I had reached the end of the fun. I wasn't sure where to go with the painting. The juice of the florescent and glitter paint seemed to have lost its excitement.

I sat down and looked at it. There was just a small portion of the top painted in wild colors and then a huge white canvas, waiting to be painted. Shit, I was stuck again.

Luckily, Chris showed up carrying her chair and sat down beside me.

"Well, what's going on here?"

I took a deep sigh, "it looks like I painted a My Little Pony Birthday Party."

I laughed.

"What's that about?"

"I have no idea, I was just letting my intuition pick the colors, and there you have it! What I would really like to talk to you about is the big blank space under it," I said.

"Okay, what about it?"

"I've been giving it some thought, okay I know I am supposed to stay out of my head, but I want to paint about a feeling, and I am not sure how to do that."

"What feeling do you want to paint?"

"Longing," I said, not sure it was a possible thing to paint.

"You do it the same way. You go to the paint table, stand there and let your intuition lead you, pick the paint, then come back here and just allow the process to begin, start painting. Don't paint with your head, just put the brush to the paper and see what appears."

That seemed easy enough, although I wasn't so sure it would work. All kinds of judgments were running through my head, doubting the process; my inner critic was screaming at me. But I put that all aside and followed Chris' instructions. I trusted her.

"I'll check in with you later," Chris said, picking up her chair and moving to the next person.

I cleaned my palette, walked into the paint table, and stood there again. I looked over the table at all the colors and different types of paint, and waited for my intuition to kick in and do some choosing. I stood there a while longer, my mind wandering off thinking about longing. I was beginning to feel sad; it was faint at first, then it grew inside my stomach, and was turning into a gnawing sort of subtle ache.

I poured a few colors of paint on my tray, almost unconsciously. I turned to walk back to my spot. As I walked down the narrow sidewalk, Chris was walking towards me. I looked at her, tears began to come to my eyes, and I was overcome with sadness.

She looked at me.

"What's happening?" she asked gently.

I blurted out, "I think I already painted about longing."

And I started crying.

She put her arms around me, "it's okay, let it out."

And I sobbed. I was remembering my sixth birthday party. It all came flooding back. My one and only birthday party.

I pushed back from Chris, and started telling her the story. It was my first birthday party and I was so excited. I had invited girls from my class at school. My parents didn't know them, but my mom had sent the invitations. My best friend Suzie was coming, along with about four other girls. I don't remember all the details, but I do remember being so happy. I remember running around outside playing, holding hands with Suzie. Then I remember my mom calling me in the house. Both my parents were standing there, and I could tell my dad was angry.

He looked at me and said, more sternly than I'd ever heard, "I don't want to ever see you holding hands with a nigger again!"

The next thing I remember everyone went home; my party was over. And, I never had another birthday party as a child, ever! Suzie was black - I never gave it a thought; she was my best friend. Even at six years old, I knew they were wrong.

I started crying again, and Chris held me.

"That is horrible," she said into my ear.

The depth of longing that came from that day is still with me. The pain I felt about Suzie and the hateful words my dad had spoken, etched in my mind and heart, knowing how wrong it was, feeling it so deeply. Then never having another birthday party, and how I longed for one. How I longed to feel loved, celebrated, and accepted. That day created a longing in me that transferred into so many other areas of my life. It was shocking to me. I had completely forgotten about this party, blocked it from my memory, and here it came to me, dressed up as a My Little Pony Birthday painting in the desert of New Mexico.

I was blown away. I didn't see it coming at all. I had a sense of grieving, letting go, and acknowledging my pain and longing. It was a flood of emotions, but it also felt like it was blowing through me. Like a flash of memory, filled with meaning and wisdom, processing, understanding, and then releasing. It was strange. There was a sensation of healing coming over me, replacing the pain with understanding and compassion.

Chris gave me a big hug and asked, "are you okay?"

I nodded.

"Are you ready to go back to the painting?"

"I think so. I'm going to try to stay with this feeling and see what comes up."

We parted, and I went back to my painting. The big blank space was still there. I sat for a while looking at it, thinking about what had just happened. I knew it no longer needed to be about longing. But I was not sure what to paint.

I decided I'd had enough for today. I needed to get away and process. There wasn't more for me to paint today. I cleaned up my space and left. We had the afternoon free, and that was just what I needed.

TWINKLING STARS

"I feel like a part of my soul has loved you since the beginning of everything. Maybe we're from the same star." - Emery Allen

Another of Chris' assistants, Laura, was presenting the evening program. She was giving a mini-workshop on "Self-Nurturing." Just exactly what I needed. It sounded like it would be loving and light. With all that I had been processing the past few days, I was ready for something light – plus, I was truly in need of learning to nurture myself.

The first time I met Laura, I felt a connection. She had a sweet, kind, loving manner about her, and you could tell she radiated acceptance. I was looking forward to her workshop.

She seemed a bit nervous when she started, but her warmth radiated into the room. I think she recognized that, and it calmed her down. We all sat in the circle, our attention fixed on her. There was a definite lightness in the air. She opened the circle, and handed out a pretty little pink booklet called "Self-Nurturing Practices - A Small Guide for Great Souls!"

Laura then began to tell us her story. She had been coming to the retreats for several years, she even is a trained facilitator, but she had a weight issue and a self-acceptance issue. Over the past year, she had lost a ton of weight and had really begun to make the transformation into owning her spirit and gifts. It was uplifting! (And sounded familiar in many ways.)

One of the things she talked about was learning to love her body again. She had always longed to lose the weight, but didn't think about what happened when the weight was gone. She was left with a lot of loose skin. Laura called them her "jiggly parts." She had created a dance to celebrate them, and she wanted us to do it all together.

The dance was simple. Just move to the music, and let your jiggly parts jiggle! Laura started the upbeat, uplifting music, and we all started laughing, dancing, and jiggling our jiggly parts. It was freeing, fun, and loving! I had never felt so accepting of myself and my body.

She then taught us all kinds of great techniques for protecting ourselves, holding on to our energy, and methods of nurturing ourselves. It was far better than I could ever have imagined. The information Laura shared was so simple, pure, and straight from her heart, plus it was deeply meaningful and useful in everyday life. It was a treasure chest of information.

Next, Laura guided us in a visualization to help us connect to our bodies. Now, I have done a lot of meditations and visualizations before, but this was like nothing I had ever tried. She started by having us connect with our internal organs - our lungs, heart, kidneys, you name it – and visualize them functioning. It was like a science experiment in biology, and as I listened I came into contact with my own body in a way I had never before. I could see it as this living, breathing machine, connecting with all its processes and recognizing it was happening inside me every moment of every day without any attention from me. It was getting me in touch with what I had painted about on my "map." This was what I had been ignoring my entire life. When I blocked out my feelings and ignored my pain, I was also ignoring this living, breathing organism that was me, my body.

This was mind blowing! It was a spiritual and physical awakening. I have always felt I was a spiritual being having a human experience, but during this visualization I realized my thinking was a mind understanding. Now I was having a body and spirit understanding - mind, body, and spirit connecting as one. I was overcome with respect and love for my body and its amazing abilities to function without any input from me, and in spite of my abusing it most of my life with food, drugs, alcohol, and more. What an awakening.

Next, Laura said she would lead us through a grounding visualization.

Before I continue, I have to give some history.

About 20 years ago I was having some major issues with my biological clock. Even though I had had a tubal ligation, there was still a ticking going on inside me. I had a longing and desire to have another baby. My only child was in college, and my husband's son was in his mid-twenties, but something inside me wanted to have a baby and I couldn't get it out of my head. My husband thought I was nuts. We were free now; we could do whatever we wanted, no more responsibility, just freedom. The thought of being tied down with a child horrified him. I was in my late thirties, he in his late forties. He wasn't going for it. I thought about adoption or foster parenting, but he was firm. And he is never firm! Part of me agreed with him; I knew I liked this freedom, but another part of me was still mourning over the lost babies, the ones I had aborted. There was guilt, shame, and regret. Mostly regret, it could fill a room. I had missed my chance. I had felt there was always going to be time, but then I was convinced by a doctor when I was so young to have the tubal ligation. I recalled the shame I felt when he told (scolded) me, "abortion is not a birth control method." That is what sealed the deal; I agreed to the tubal ligation. Now all that remained was regret. Regret for having the abortions, regret for having my tubes tied, and regret that I let a doctor make a decision about such an important aspect of my life. And, it was too late to have it be any different. I had to come to terms with it.

For weeks I moped around, struggling to pull myself out of this depressed state. Finally, one day I decided that I needed to let it go, process it, and paint. Painting or creating art was always my go-to method of working through painful memories. I went to the art supply store and bought a big canvas. As I prepared, an idea started coming to me. I saw in my mind an angel throwing three stars into the sky. It would represent me allowing the spirit of those three babies to forever shine in the night sky. I started painting and it all came together. It took me a few days, but when it was done it was exactly perfect. The angel that represented me was peaceful and ethereal looking, and the stars were large and filled the dark, sparkly sky of the canvas. They were painted in bright yellow with gold edges, with rays radiating from them that made it seem like they were glowing. It was a cathartic experience; I had been processing my feelings with each brush stroke. When it was completed, I felt I was too. I had come to terms with these lost babies, and allowed myself to grieve and forgive myself. It was so healing. That picture hung on the wall for many years. Every time I looked at it, I remembered their sweet spirits and it felt good, until it didn't anymore. One day, I realized that it was over. I didn't need to keep looking it; it was done for me. So, I took the picture down. I never thought about this picture again. My heart had been healed. Or so I thought.

Now, back to the Pinon Room. Laura is getting ready to lead us in a guided visualization to help us get grounded and connect spiritually. She starts by asking us to stand. She then told us to close our eyes, and imagine our bare feet are touching the earth. Imagine this direct contact, and feel the coolness of the earth; nothing else matters except this connection between our feet and the earth.

I feel that I have gone to another space and time; I am standing barefoot in the glorious desert of New Mexico, the red dirt and my feet becoming one.

Laura tells us to imagine that our feet are sprouting roots and the roots are digging into the earth, going deeper and deeper.

My feet feel big and wide, and the sprouts of roots are going in all directions. I can sense the coolness of the earth and I am becoming one with it.

Then, Laura tells us to imagine the roots come up our legs and we begin to grow branches, and the branches begin to grow and reach out in every direction.

I am totally feeling it; it is like I am in a trance, and everything she describes is happening to me.

I feel the roots into the earth, my branches growing in every direction, and I am getting bigger and fuller.

Next, Laura says let your branches reach higher, let them go into the sky, and out into the universe.

My heart is opening wide and the feeling is like I have never felt before.

Suddenly, my branches are reaching out and I see three painted stars - the exact three stars that I painted 20 years ago. They are shining so brightly. The memory of painting the stars floods my mind and at the same time, my branches, which now looked more like vines, are beginning to wrap around them.

I had totally forgotten about the painting and the stars. When I saw them in this vision, it felt like an electrical shock. Then the vines completely embraced the three stars, wrapping fully around them, the sky brightened, and it was like a spark erupted. The connection between the branches and the stars became electric and had a glow around them. A current of energy flowed through them, down the vines, into the branches, and entered my body and my heart. Along with the feeling came a sense of knowing; it was like they were talking to me without words.

They were saying, "it's all right, it's perfect, we love you, love, love, love."

And the most powerful feeling of unconditional love filled my body and radiated through the vines between me and the stars. I was just basking in this indescribably powerful feeling of love.

I had stopped listening to Laura, and just allowed myself to stay in the experience. Tears ran down my face. I was amazed at seeing the painted stars, long forgotten, and I knew this was about healing. The love that was flowing into me was so powerful, so pure that I knew this moved beyond old actions here on earth, and came from another place. Everything was exactly as it should be, and love abounded. I was completely filled with a sense of love, forgiveness, and acceptance like I had never experienced before. Time and space had transformed, and I was embraced in the most beautiful love I had ever felt.

Slowly, nearly like slow motion, it started to fade. I was being called back.

I heard Laura say, "breathe slowly and deeply, and bring yourself back into the room."

It took me a few moments to compose myself, and I sat down in my chair. I was still overcome by emotion, and the radiating energy of the shower of love.

Afterwards, I was sort of dumbfounded and didn't know what to say to anyone. I felt like I had experienced something transformative and otherworldly, but I didn't think I could put it into words, let alone have anyone understand. I was trying to get my mind around how those stars, painted 20 years ago and long forgotten, just appeared like magic. The whole thing just freaked me out a bit, and combined with the other events that had been happening since I arrived, I was sure I was in some kind of alternative universe.

Chris had told us she had been holding these retreats here for 14 years because of the magic and sacredness of this place. I'd have to agree with her!

And I remembered Russ from Santa Fe who told me, "There is magic out there."

They were both right!

A group of us walked back to our rooms together, everyone going on about how wonderful it had been. Me included. Laura was something else! A real gift. There was a lightness in my step, and a warmness in my heart!

When I arrived at my screen door, something hit me. I looked in, and realized that I couldn't sleep another night like I had been. It was like I was taken over by something, and I started moving the furniture around. I put the nightstands and lamps on top of the beds, shoved the beds around, and reconfigured the room. I moved one bed into a corner, out of the range of the porch light, and the other one against the wall by the window. I moved both nightstands on either side of my new bed location, and put the lamps on them. I remade the bed, and used an old beach towel I had with me as a rug.

Within minutes, the room had been transformed. The feeling was entirely different. I laid down on the bed to try it out. The porch light did not shine anywhere near the bed. The door was at my side and the window was at my feet, so I was tucked into a corner, which felt cozy and safer. Why hadn't I thought of this before? It even felt cooler; how was that possible?

THE LABYRINTH

"Labyrinths offer the opportunity to walk in meditation to that place within us where the rational merges with the intuitive and the spiritual is reborn." - Etched in a rock

Waking up with a big stretch, I realized it was morning and I had slept through the night. As a matter of fact, I had slept soundly and comfortably. What a change! I felt renewed and happy. I had done Feng Shui on my room, and didn't even know it. I looked at the clock on my phone, and realized I had slept in and had better get going; breakfast would be over in a few minutes! This was going to be a good day.

After breakfast, I decided to walk the labyrinth. I followed the trail past the Pinon Room, beside the donkey corral, and past the Zen garden. It wasn't too far until the path turned off to the right towards the labyrinth. I had walked out there several times, never having enough time to fully experience it. The labyrinth was at the base of my favorite mountain at the Ghost Ranch. Shrubs and trees surrounded it, and the labyrinth was laid out with rocks; at the center were several big boulders. The sign said it was a half-mile walk, around and around. It was a quiet and still morning, with some rain clouds hanging in the sky. It felt so peaceful and serene. There wasn't another person in sight.

I read the information posted on the sign. It suggested you meditate on a thought or question before you begin the walk and ask any spirit guides, angels, goddesses, or whatever you believed in, to join you. Again, being that I had promised to be open to anything, I stood at the entrance and imagined a group of invisible guides floating around me. Then I began to focus on self-acceptance and loving my body. I did that for a few minutes, and then began to walk very slowly. I lowered my eyes towards the ground, and pulled back my shoulders, taking slow, deep breaths. The quietness seemed to grow, and the sound of the gravel beneath my feet seemed incredibly loud. The awareness made me walk slower and lighter.

I kept the idea of self-acceptance in my thoughts as I made the twists and turns towards the center of the labyrinth.

The word GRACE came to me again, floating into my head, "Be all with grace, allow your gifts to come forward with grace."

I continued to walk and let that word stay with me.

After a few more turns, the word INTEGRATION came to me. I let it swim around in my mind, and I understood it was time to bring myself together into one whole. I repeated it over and over, and recognized it was about connecting my heart, soul, and body and living in my full being. Living in my full being! That was it! Living integrated fully in body, mind, and soul. Being

respectful of my body, connecting with my essence, and using my mind as a tool to help me navigate in the world. Having a voice that is true, not angry, not scared, not apologetic, but just my grace intertwined with my wisdom, compassion, and spiritual essence. Owning all aspects of myself, and especially embracing the divine feminine. I let this all ruminate as I continued to walk.

As I was making my way around the last quarter of the labyrinth, the words, "living small is making you large" came into my consciousness.

I repeated the words, "living small is making you large."

It hit me like a ton of bricks. Wow, I got it. Living small encompasses so many concepts and ideas, but includes shame, regret, and longing. All the things that dampen my power, and keep it focused on my (alleged) faults. Living small makes me turn to food for comfort, engulfs me in self-pity, and allows me to minimize my positive traits and gifts. When I am living small, I can't see the greatness of my spirit.

"Living small is making you large," were the words I needed to hear to snap me into consciousness.

All the events of this retreat and my trip so far had been about me opening to my largeness, and this wasn't about the size of my body!

As I finished the walk and returned to the opening of the labyrinth, I felt new insights and understanding. I stood there for a moment letting it sink in. Grace, Integration, Living Small is Making Me Large. The labyrinth and whoever accompanied me had helped me see things in a whole new way.

I headed back to the Pinon Room for our morning session, walking with my head held higher and a lightness in my step.

CHANNELING WONDER WOMAN

"Do you really want to look back on your life and see how wonderful it could have been had you not been afraid to live it?" - Caroline Myss

The morning movement was freestyle dancing. We formed a circle, and one by one each of us had to get in the center and lead the dance; whatever we did, the group did. When we left the circle, we chose who would dance next. It was lively, and we were all laughing, but it was also intimidating to have all eyes on you, mimicking your movements.

Twice I was picked to go next, and I had to say, "I already went."

It made me feel invisible. It was a weird feeling, particularly after my experience at the labyrinth.

We broke off in twos for the next exercise. My partner was Connie, a young woman who I had immediately connected with on the first day. Chris told us we were doing the Wonder Woman exercise.

We had to stand with our hands on our hips in the Wonder Woman stance, and say proudly, "I am ___." And you could fill in the blank with any word you felt described you.

Your partner was to respond, "I see you as ____."

It was very powerful. I said things like I am beautiful, I am strong, I am wise, I am creative, I am loving, I am spirit, I am God, I am compassionate, etc.

My partner said each of them back to me, "I see you are strong. I see you are beautiful."

Then we reversed.

Afterwards she said to me, "I kept waiting for you to say, 'I am here.' It feels like you aren't being seen."

When she spoke these words, it nearly took my breath away and I suddenly noticed a tightening in my throat. She saw a truth that I had been hiding from. I don't feel seen. Not the real me. I didn't know if it was even possible. I had spent my life hiding behind some persona or another. Earlier in the week one of the other participants had talked about playing roles. She said she spent her life playing the role that fit other people's movies, whatever role they wanted her to play. That's what I had been doing my entire life.

How could I be seen? I never move through the world as myself; I just play whatever role fits whatever situation. Plus, I never wanted anyone to see the "real" me. Because I saw myself as damaged, worthless, and ashamed. Memories of being molested as a kid flooded forward and how much shame and fear I had about it. I felt that if people looked too closely at me they would see it, they would know the horribleness of me - the dirty shameful thing I tried so desperately to hide.

Most of my life I had been hiding that shame, although I had years of therapy and felt healed in so many other ways. I never realized this was still hanging on. I had created a set of personalities and personas so that part of me would stay hidden. What I realized this day was that the wounded, molested kid was not the "real" me, the real me was all those things I declared in the Wonder Woman exercise. The real me was the layer beneath the shame, the true essence of me, this unique spirit was the one who needed and so desperately wanted to be seen.

I thought of all the encounters I had with my higher self this week, the God essence of who I was. That was the real me. It was time! Time to move from behind the shame and stand in my true essence in my Wonder Woman power, without excuses. Just be me.

Hell yes! This stuff is powerful! I was so grateful to Connie for being honest with me.

The transition back to painting was hard after that experience. I was filled with new thoughts; there was so much to process. I sat down in the chair in my little outdoor studio and stared off at the mountains and brilliant blue sky. It was quiet again; all the women were back at their stations working away. I sat there for a while, soaking in the beauty and thinking about the morning's circle. What amazing things were happening to me! There were openings in my life I never expected, issues that I had long forgotten, and healing that I never expected. As I thought about it, most of these issues had totally lost all their power inside me. The abortions came to mind; I felt healed. My sixth birthday party and the deep longing; I felt healed. The not being seen part and the fear of people finding out I had been molested - the power that had held over me seemed to have evaporated. Coming to terms with the concept of the real me, it felt clear, honest, and true. How could I be processing so much and feel so healed? It was miraculous! The Wonder Woman exercise was so empowering, physically standing with my hands on my hips and declaring my power transformed me. I felt inspired.

I needed to paint. I got up, took my tray, and loaded it with paint. I knew exactly what to pick. Back at my canvas, I started painting over the My Little Pony Birthday Party and drew the shape of a woman; it nearly filled the entire canvas. I had her standing in the Wonder Woman pose, hands on hips. Then I started painting her hair, bright pearlescent aqua blue in squiggles out from her head filling the upper portion of the paper, nearly covering the previous painting. The body of the woman was bright yellow. I painted the glorious mountains and sky behind her. It was a big painting and it took some time; it filled up the entire afternoon painting session.

Before long, it was time to head to the cafeteria. I cleaned up, headed to dinner, and then back to my room for a rest.

That evening was another evening session with Chris at her casita. As I lay on my bed, trying to regroup and relax, I wasn't sure I was up to any more insights or breakthroughs. I was pretty exhausted. The idea of not going sounded good, but I kept remembering my promise to give my all. This was a unique opportunity, and I had to go for it. Things were happening and I wanted to bust though as much as I could.

I met my neighbors, and we headed up the hill. It was raining, so we all huddled under our umbrellas for the walk. It was so good to laugh, and talk about our insights and things our paintings had taught us. We had all settled into a nice rhythm of our daily activities and time together. It felt good. I was beginning to feel so close to these women, a bond that was hard to describe. We all were a bit apprehensive about the session ahead, but were also eager to explore more about ourselves and learn more about each other.

Chris started at seven, sharp. Again, each person had 15 minutes to share and five minutes for feedback. One by one, we shared and gave each other open and honest feedback. At times, it felt so still you could hear a pin drop; other times were filled with laughter. I was so glad I came. When it was my turn, I knew what I wanted to talk about - being seen.

"Today, Connie helped me so much. In the Wonder Woman exercise this morning she gave me some feedback that opened me up. She said she wanted me to say 'I am Here.' She felt I needed to be seen. And, she was right! I don't feel seen. Even at the circle dance this morning, two people picked me to go and I had already gone; it was like they never saw me in the circle."

I was flooded with emotion, but continued.

"Early this morning I walked the labyrinth, and that was amazing. I really got in touch with a lot of stuff. Between that and the Wonder Woman thing, I am really feeling my own power!"

Then I remembered I had brought the description I had written of who I want to be that Chris had asked me the second morning to write.

"Chris, I brought the description of what I think makes a powerful woman. Can I read it? I asked.

"Of course," she responded. "But please stand up to read it."

I stood up and began to read from my phone.

"Calm, peaceful, and even-tempered. Exudes a quality of wisdom and power - but with a foundation of loving-kindness. She is secure in her knowledge and beliefs, and will gently share when the time is right. Self-confident, self-aware, and spiritually connected. She practices sacred selfishness and knows how to set boundaries with ease. She is strong and faces fear head on. She embodies her essence with grace, ease, and charm. Truly authentic in body, mind, and spirit. There is a completeness that feels real and true - from voice, demeanor, beliefs, and even the way she dresses. Open, self-assured, loving, and aware. Living life is a practice of her deepest knowing."

"Take a deep breath and stand still for a moment," Chris suggested. "Tell me what that felt like reading that description?"

"Good. Well, actually, really great," I responded.

"Did you feel that it described you?"

"Yes, I guess so, I would like to think I could be that," I answered with a little doubt.

"Do you realize you couldn't write those things unless you were those things?" Chris stated confidently, looking directly into my eyes.

"I never thought of it like that," I said, "I guess that's true."

I hadn't ever thought of that before. Where had that description come from? I wrote it quickly; it just flowed. How did I know that was who I wanted to be?

"Well, how about you tell us something, just say anything, but be her. Be that person you described," Chris requested.

My heart started pounding, and I could feel my throat tightening up. I didn't know if I could do it or not. But, I knew I had to. I stood straight and started talking. The first thing that came to mind was my walk around the labyrinth and I shared that, talking about what a spiritual experience it had been. I tried to channel the person I described - self-assured, peaceful, confident, but not prideful, yet gentle, graceful and wise. It was a lot to embrace. It felt magnificent! Scary, but wonderful.

I finished and sat down quickly. I felt a flush cross my face and my skin felt hot. Then Chris asked if I wanted feedback; I nodded yes. All the remarks and feedback were validating and empowering. Although I felt exposed in a way I never have before, kind of raw. My inner critic was starting in on me with judgment, criticism, and shame, but I just ignored her and brought myself back to the present moment and let their kind words embrace me.

As I lay in bed that night, before falling asleep, it was impossible not to think about the events of the day. Beneath all the insights and emotions, I had a sense of peace. There was a part of me that knew something big was happening. I tried to think about some of my issues, and there was no energy for them at all; it was like they had been erased and no longer held any power. It was a little mind-boggling, but I liked it.

I thought about the next day, the last full day at the retreat. I had to think about what I wanted to take away. It was who I want to BE, not what I had to DO from this point forward. What would it look like if I stepped into my own power? Not some angry power, like, "I'm not gonna let them push around anymore," kind of thing. But real spiritual power. The things I have learned here about truth, grace, and gratitude, and really being seen. That is something else altogether. That's what I wanted.

Yes, I could see it now; it was definitely a possibility. Actually, a strong probability.

Owning the Truth

"Truth is like the sun. You can shut it out for a time, but it ain't goin' away." - Elvis Presley

I woke up from a dream. It seemed so real. I was on a boat and was jetting around through the water, standing up, feeling strong, hands on the wheel, guiding the boat through the water at a fast speed. The boat was bouncing on top of the water, leaving big waves in its wake. It felt like I was in charge, carefree, and independent. Somehow, I knew I was headed for a dock near Los Angeles. I knew my destination was Mood Fabrics.

I laughed out loud. My dream was about driving a speedboat to Mood Fabrics! The idea of it was just funny!

That's what the trip was about, me seeking some authentic part of me. Over the past few days, in my downtime I'd been sketching clothing and jewelry designs, something I hadn't done in years! And I'd been thinking about different fabrics and styles. Somehow this was all playing out in my dreams. The first afternoon, when I started sketching clothes, it seemed very odd, but I just got into it. It was as if I was designing a new style, a new look that connected with the part of me who was beneath all the layers – the woman who stood up at the casita last night and shared the experience at the labyrinth.

I lay there thinking about it, actually feeling a bit superficial, but then realizing that was part of the hiding and not being seen, and the personas I have created all require a look that suits them. Even the way I dressed said so much about me, and it was time to change that too. That's what the sketching was about, and this dream. Standing strong in my own power and being authentic in every way possible, even the clothes I wear.

That got me thinking about all the beautiful fabric and beads I had been collecting for most of my life. They were all stored away in boxes and hidden in cabinets, waiting for me to do something with them. But I was always waiting, saving them. Saving them for what? It occurred to me that now was the time to use them. Why in the world should I keep hiding them? It was time to go through it all, use the things that I love, and get rid of the rest.

Another thought occurred to me; I could hire someone to make the clothes that I had sketched. There was a woman who taught pattern making and sewing classes at the local college. There must be a student she knows who wants to make some money. I knew how to sew, but didn't enjoy it, so why not hire someone who does?

My head starting spinning with ideas. Right then, I so wanted to get on the internet and start researching things. Then I remembered; I was unplugged. Yes, there was no way to do that. I'd heard from some of the women that there was Wi-Fi in the library; I was tempted to head over there.

Then I remembered I was here to experience this retreat, and my mind was running in the direction of distraction. Slow down. This was all good information, but it could wait until I got home. There was more work to do here.

My next thought was about painting and what I wanted to process. What I really wanted to do was let go of the living small identity that no longer fit. I realized that I could drop it like a hot potato. The only thing holding me back was me. I now have a definition of who I want to be - a peaceful, graceful, creative, loving, and spiritually connected person. So, why not own it and let go of feeling ashamed and broken? I can release that victimhood role and all the stories that go along with it. I am bigger than all that.

If I believe, and I do, that all of that was part of what I came into this life to experience and learn from, then it is time for me to rejoice and recognize that I have learned those lessons and I am ready to live. Playing small is just bullshit! It is the residue that I am holding onto out of familiarity and false sense of security. What is the worst thing that could happen if I let go of my story?

Well, I would have to take responsibility for my life, use my voice, speak my truth, and set boundaries. Honor myself. That has been the missing piece. My fear of having to be responsible for my own power, my connection to the great oneness, seemed too scary because I didn't feel that I had the skills to take care of myself. It was like driving that speedboat in my dream. You have to feel confident with that kind of power to stand up, take the wheel, and drive.

That's it, an "ah ha" moment! What was keeping me stuck was being bound in the people pleasing mode, putting others needs before my own, and staying stuck in my same old stories of victimhood. Plus, the biggest one of all - not allowing myself to resonate with the perfection of my being and my connection to the great oneness.

One thing this week has taught me is that I am enough; we are all enough just as we are. The constant seeking for perfection, or looking outward for some solution to a problem, is a waste of time. It all starts with recognizing that inside we are perfect in every way, whole and complete. We are exactly where we need to be, doing exactly what we need to be doing. It is a matter of stepping back into our bigger self, and staying present. Standing up, tall and confident, and driving that powerboat with the wake foaming out behind me, knowing I have the power! That's it! That's the gift! That's the real TRUTH!

The End is Just the Beginning

"You are one of a kind. A never before, a never again. You're here for a reason that didn't exist before and won't ever again." - Author Unknown

The time seemed to have flown by, and here we were at our final morning of the retreat. Our morning movement was freestyle dancing to some amazing music. It was a song I knew well by Libby Roderick called "How Could Anyone?" The lyrics began:

> *How could anyone ever tell you*
> *You were anything less than beautiful?*
> *How could anyone ever tell you*
> *You were less than whole?*
> *How could anyone fail to notice*
> *That your loving is a miracle?*
> *How deeply you're connected to my soul?*

It's a beautiful song with a beautiful melody. It had moved me years earlier when I first heard it, and it moved me more this morning. I sang it as I moved to the music; it felt so good, so free. I had lost the inhibitions I had had earlier in the week, and now I just moved however and wherever I felt. I danced outside and twirled around in the clearing in front of the Pinon Room, feeling the openness and the fresh, clean air. I let the beat dictate my movements. We must have danced 10 minutes before Chris rang the bell, signaling us to return to the room.

We all gathered and stood in a big circle. Chris explained that our final exercise was one of connection. One person would get in the middle of the circle, the rest of us would stand around them, and the person in the middle would make eye contact with one person at a time until the circle was complete. She asked us to hold eye contact until we were really sure it felt complete. If this had been one of the first exercises it would have been extremely difficult, but now, after days of being together and getting to know each person on such a sacred level, this felt wonderful. Just holding eye contact with each person was so profound; it was intimate and moving.

When my turn came, I got in the center and decided I would just concentrate on the meaning of Namaste - the God in me sees the God in you. I found myself feeling something deep from inside as I looked into each person's eyes. It was recognition of our connection and oneness. It was so powerful. It was a feeling of connecting on a true soul level.

We left the circle and headed back to our paintings; this was our final chance to paint. There was energy in the air - part excitement, part melancholy. This was the end, our final time in this holy process together. The day would end with an art show, where each of us would have the opportunity to explain our paintings. When I got back to my little area, there was the big yellow woman with wild aqua hair waiting for me. I looked at her and realized there was much to be done. I knew the rest of this painting was about standing in my power, and this woman with her hands on her hips was just what I needed.

At first, I thought I would list my powers, my gifts, and then I realized that was pointless. It was about so much more than that. I had come to a deeper understanding. My journey here has been filled with twists and turns, drama and stories, awakenings, and learning truths about myself. It was time for me to let go of all the facades and hold onto what was real - the truth that I am already everything I need. I don't need to be fixed; I am whole and compete. I can move forward, step into my own power, and live each day fully and wholly. *That* is what this woman should represent.

I filled my palette tray with paint, and started to embellish her. First, I painted power bracelets on her wrists, just like Wonder Woman. Then I began to paint the symbols of the seven chakras on each of the energy centers. At her feet, I painted roots going from the earth and wrapping around her legs as a symbol of being grounded. Out of the top of her head, I painted lines with purple sparkle paint reaching towards the sky as a symbol of her connection to the higher realms. I painted the background all black and wrote in big purple letters, "I AM." Reminding me, "I am that; I am!" I am part of the bigger oneness, a wave in the ocean.

The final challenge was the face. The day before I had painted the face, and then hated it and covered it with gesso.

When Chris saw what I did, she told me, "No, you can't repaint the face! You must go with your original face."

I thought about this and realized I had to release judgment. So somehow, I had to recreate the original face. It was hard to do; my inner critic really wanted me to "fix" it. But I resisted, and recreated the same face as best as I could. The eyes were too far apart, the nose was way too big, and the mouth just looked weird. But, I just let it go. This was my woman in all her glory.

I looked at the throat and realized I had painted a bright open 5th chakra, with rays radiating up and down signifying the flow that now existed. The flow from the high spiritual realms was connected to my lower physical being. It was clear that my throat was open, and my heart was able to connect my body and spirit fully.

I began to weep. Never had I felt so whole and complete. I knew this painting was done. I sat down, and continued to look at her for a long time. This wasn't a masterpiece, it wasn't intended to be one, but it represented so much. It was the culmination of my time here and what I had learned about myself. This big yellow, powerful, and strong woman standing in her Wonder Woman pose. Her head was held high, her feet grounded in the earth, her 7th chakra extending and connecting to the heavens. All the chakras were spinning together in harmony, especially the throat chakra.

I had found my voice, and connected with my authentic self, below the layers of false personas and people pleasing ways. She represented healing and strength, and as I looked at her I felt it deep within my soul. It may look a bit childish to others, but to me it had great meaning. Yes, it definitely felt complete.

It was hard to break down my little painting studio; it had felt like a sanctuary this week. This retreat was coming to an end, and it was hard to let go. Chris' assistants asked that we find a spot on the walls and hang all our paintings together. They would be setting up for the art show this evening. I found a spot, hung up my paintings, cleaned up my mess, helped clean up the bigger space, and then took off for some final time outdoors in the beautiful, sacred land of the Ghost Ranch.

I stood outside the Pinon Room and took a deep breath. I looked around; there is a sense of the sacred in every direction. I decided to head back to the labyrinth and walk it one last time. I crossed the small bridge, followed the dirt trail heading towards the Zen garden, and walked slowly, enjoying every moment in touch with this space.

The connection I had with New Mexico is hard to describe, but felt real and deep. Everything about the land and the sky called to me.

Before long, I was back at the labyrinth. At the entrance were a big rock and a bench. I sat on the bench and just took it all in. I wanted to absorb as much of this energy as I could. My body felt tingly.

With every breath I took, I felt a deeper and deeper connection. The solitude added to the feeling. There were so many people at the Ghost Ranch, but not one in sight. It felt like I was alone in the middle of nowhere. Just me and God.

I sat completely quiet and focused on my breathing; I became as present as possible and just immersed myself in the moment - the connection, the sacredness of the land, this magical labyrinth, and the absolute quiet. Some part of me knew I was imprinting myself with this memory so it would be available to me in the future. It was feelings of bliss, absolute connection, and peace. It filled my heart with joy, and warmth spread through my body. Being present, not thinking ahead, or worrying about the past, just truly being totally present had a power that was beyond limits. Time stood still.

I looked up and saw three large birds floating on the air currents just above the labyrinth, their majesty and beauty intensifying my experience. I was transfixed watching them. There was no sound, just the graceful and elegant flight of birds swooping up and down and back and forth. I'm not sure how long I sat there; time had escaped me. I never walked the labyrinth that afternoon; I just sat on that bench having a moment with New Mexico and God.

Unveiling our Souls - The Art Show

"Be creative. Feed your soul. Love your life!" - Chris Zydel

When I walked into the Pinon Room that evening, it had been transformed. It looked like an art show. Chris' assistants had hung spotlights around the room, so that all the artwork was emphasized and glowed. It felt special, beautiful, and sacred.

It was time for each of us to share our process and work. We had painted silently, in a type of meditative state, without giving feedback or receiving any, other than our time spent with Chris. This would be our first opportunity to really share our work. Many of the women had dressed up, which I never thought to do. But their dressing up made it feel more special and festive.

We gathered together while Chris explained the process. One by one, we would go to the art displays. Each person had the option to speak; we could talk about our paintings, our process, or anything we felt like sharing. Talking about our paintings wasn't required. If you did speak, then the group could give feedback - if you chose to receive it. There was a sense of excitement and anticipation. Chris asked if anyone would volunteer to go first. One woman raised her hand, her art the closest to where we stood.

We each grabbed a folding chair and circled around her. She began to share her painting process and her story. It was rich with symbolism and expression of her innermost feelings and experiences. She set the tone for the depth and level of intimacy for the evening. We were all drawn further into the sacredness of the process.

All week long we had been watching each other paint, seeing amazing works of art being uncovered, without any understanding of the meaning, the depth, or the process behind them. This was a look into our lives - the heartache, the joy and sorrow, a rawness that is rarely available for others' eyes. We moved our chairs around the rooms, focusing on each woman as she told her story and shared her art. Some paintings were dark and mysterious, others bright and beautiful, all of them filled with symbolism. Each woman had a unique and diverse story, deep, meaningful, and so sacred.

When it was my turn, I stood up, not sure what to say. An old feeling of self-consciousness welled up through me, as I remembered the fearful feeling I used to have that people could see the shame I was hiding. I knew in my head it was not relevant today, especially after everything I had learned here, but it was my auto-response when standing in front of a group of people. The women were all seated in a big circle around me, their eyes and attention fixed on me. I suddenly felt like a cartoon character from a kids' show my daughter used to watch, Henrietta Hippo. She was big, very chubby, and she wore a tutu that was way too small. My shirt felt like it was too small, and my belly was too big, my ankles too small, and my head felt like a peanut. I was flooded with all kinds of weird feelings. It felt like I was having an out-of-body experience. This was all going through my head in a matter of seconds. I began to realize this was old stuff, the stuff I had come here to face - this autopilot response of self-consciousness and fear. Wanting to be seen, but then feeling self-conscious and shy. It felt crazy, and it felt like it didn't fit any longer. I have no idea how long I stood there processing all this in my head. It may have been seconds, but it felt like minutes had passed. I knew I had been hiding most of my life, filled with fear and shame. But right then, I knew it was over.

Suddenly, I began to speak.

"When I signed up to come here, my original plan was to come find out why I kept sabotaging myself. I started things full speed ahead, but then as I got closer to success I would always find a way to swerve off in another direction. Then I'd go about beating myself for failing yet another thing. This was a pattern throughout my entire life. Then, I found out I had this tumor in my throat and things shifted. It became my new focus, healing the issues related to my throat chakra. Little did I know they would all be connected."

I took a breath.

"Honestly, when I came here I didn't know what to expect. I knew it was about painting, intuitive painting, and I was excited about experiencing it. But some part of me thought I would find some inner artist, and I would head home afterwards with a new passion for painting. That's not at all what happened. Painting here this week unlocked things inside, cracked me open, healed me. I have processed so much here and worked through it with such speed, it is shocking. I am still processing and probably will be for the near future. I feel blessed."

Then I described each painting, and what it represented for me. My first painting. The paintings with the big blue and green circles (representing my gifts and strengths), with the red circle (representing my heart) and all the lines, (representing blood veins), that connected them all together, giving the flow of life to each circle. The veins representing a new understanding and re-connection, and it all becoming one.

At first it seemed so simple and mundane, almost childlike, but it turned into such meaning for me. It symbolized a reconnection to my spirit and all the gifts I came here to express, ones I had been ignoring, disowning, and downplaying most of my life. The process of painting turned a few simple circles into a deeply meaningful, and spiritual, awakening.

Next was my 1960's poster map. I explained how it depicted the process of how I ended up with the problems in my throat. It was the visual representation of creating illness. But it was also a map of discovery and understanding. It guided me through the denial I had been in for decades, and helped me see the system I had created to hide my light. How I was trained from an early age to put my own needs last, becoming hyper attentive to my environment and outwardly focused, and building a set of unhealthy copping behaviors. The entire process of painting this map was like one giant light bulb moment. It just kept illuminating issue after issue, piece by piece, until I really saw the entire picture. My life played out in my throat! It allowed me to take a look at a lifetime of habits and behaviors that were making me sick and keeping me from connecting with my light, the true, authentic me. Doing this in just a couple of days with a 20-inch by 36-inch painting seemed mind-boggling!

And, finally, the My Little Pony birthday party/Wonder Woman painting. I had to admit it looked a little weird at first, but I loved the final product. It represented the turning point and the shift from being a victim to becoming empowered. Standing in my own power, driving the speedboat! However, it wasn't the final product that was important - it was the process I went through with this painting that opened me up on so many levels, especially the healing I had over my sixth birthday party and its connection to longing. I deeply understood how one event can set in motion a lifetime feeling, which becomes attached to so much more and grows into a big deep hole that couldn't be filled.

I also learned that healing only takes a nanosecond when it is done on a soul level. That's what happened to me. The healing of longing, which I would never have guessed started with that party, connected a chain of events and beliefs, like a spark on a fuse, which exploded simultaneously in a matter of minutes. Then, from that original painting, the My Little Pony birthday party, came Wonder Woman. It was me symbolically owning my power and standing tall, with all my energy centers in balance, rooted in the earth, and connected to the universe. Hands on hips, with magical bracelets able to protect me in times of trouble. This painting brought the process full circle.

When I finished, I paused and looked at the group. I felt happy to be part of this amazing experience.

Just then, one of the women said, "hey, her hair looks like a peacock!"

I laughed, and then looked at the painting and it was true! I hadn't seen it until she noticed it. The aqua blue squiggly hair, with the rays coming out of the top of her head towards the heavens, did look like a peacock. My new power animal! It was more symbolism of my transformation. Unconsciously, I had included a peacock in my painting.

I got some really nice feedback, and that felt good. But I don't think I vocalized, or truly understood, how much of a transformation I had experienced. It was too soon; I was still processing and trying to get my head around all that had transpired.

And it wasn't over yet. Soon, even more would be revealed to me.

After everyone shared, we had to dismantle the art show, roll up our paintings, and leave the Pinon Room for good. The sacred space we had created just a few short days ago was slowly being morphed back into the plain old room it had been before we arrived. I thought about what Chris and the others had manifested here, how the mood was set, how each of the women brought some part of the sacred with them, and together we made this place holy. It had become a safe space to explore scary places kept hidden for years, even decades. It had become a sanctuary for opening up and healing, and a place to learn about self-care.

The slogan, "Needy, greedy and proud of it" rang through the rooms during the week.

It was an environment of acceptance and non-judgment, of tranquility and mediation. How had that all been here one minute, and then suddenly this very same space returned to just a simple room?

As I headed back to the Staffhouse, I felt like I was floating. My physical body was walking but a bigger part of me lost in thought, looking into the dark sky and the bright stars. It was clear that something magical was happening to me. Whatever it was, I was ready!

Saying Goodbye (to Cindy)

"The beginning of wisdom is to call things by their right names." - Proverb

Morning came too quickly. This was it; it was over. We were all meeting for breakfast and then going our separate ways. How had the time gone by so fast? The idea of going back to the real world seemed foreign, yet I could feel myself being pulled back. I was thinking of making a few phone calls, writing a Facebook post, and the day of travel ahead. I had one foot in this sacred place, and one foot back into life.

It was early still, so I decided to pack up my car and go for one last walk in this magical place. It didn't take too long to get my stuff in order, pack the car, and rearrange the room back to the way I had found it.

When I was done, I stood looking at the room. When I first arrived, I remember being shocked at the stark simplicity and feeling the dreaded heat wave. I remembered being scared and hardly sleeping at all the first night.

Today, I saw something completely different. I felt sad leaving this little room. It had become a cocoon, a place to process, journal, and sketch. A private place where all I had to think about was me. No interruptions, demands, or expectations. It represented all of that. The heat had subsided, and the bed had miraculously transformed into a comfortable, soft place. The space felt cozy, and I had been sleeping soundly. I was going to miss this room. I took one final look, and headed out to soak in as much of the spirit of this place as I could before I hit the road.

As I took off down the path, I had a lightness in my step; I actually felt like skipping. It was so beautiful and quiet, the sun just peeking out over the mountains. The stillness, the warmth, and the smell of rain in the air took me back. I could feel it on my skin, a memory. It seemed weird, but I could sense myself as a little girl. Like I was actually transported back in time. I felt that skip in my step, along with the feeling in the air, the sky.

I don't know if it was a memory or if it was imagined from an old photograph my mom has in her house, but I could see myself all dressed up for Easter. I had a white pinafore with a big ruffled skirt, a yellow eyelet dress beneath it. I had white lace edged socks and Mary Janes, a white hat with yellow daisies, and white gloves on my hands. I was skipping through the desert in a field of wildflowers. It was like I was looking back in time at her, but it also seemed like now. She seemed so innocent and pure.

I could hear my mom saying, "you look like a living doll!"

The words "living doll" rang in my head. I know it was just a saying, but it was more than that. Suddenly my feelings began to shift, and I stopped and took in a big breath of fresh air. That little girl, me, was a living doll. My mom dressed me like I was a living, breathing doll. I became the image of what she imagined in her head - the family she wanted, the look she wanted to convey to the outside world. For me, it was the beginning of disconnecting from myself, my essence, and my spirit.

I realized this memory was about how step by step, dress by dress, action by action I became what other people wanted me to be, forgetting who I really was. I realized that my mom still longed for that cute little girl, her "living doll." I was still trying to please her and everyone else, and failing miserably. That little girl wasn't who I am, and never has been.

Sadness rushed through me. On a deep level I knew this, and had known it for a long time. But this morning was like I was mourning the end of her. I was letting her go once and for all. She is my mom's dream girl, not who I am. It all felt very weird. That entire memory surprised me, the physical sensations, the truth, my disconnect, and my mom's dreams and desires for me. It felt awkward and uncomfortable, yet so real. It was hard to face, but I had always known. I wasn't the little girl she dreamed of, I never was, and never would be.

This was part of my journey here, part of my healing, part of the reason I had the tumor in my throat. It was time for me to come to terms with it, to stop hating myself for not being something I could never be, and to stop trying to get her approval. I wasn't that little girl, and it was time I stepped into my authentic power and owned it once and for all.

The skipping had stopped, and I was slowly walking near my favorite mountain. Still deep in thought, I began to feel the warmth of the sun on my face and became aware of the surroundings. What a strange experience. This truth of our relationship was always there, but both of us had been ignoring it my entire life. I could ignore it no longer.

Suddenly, I realized my stomach was growling fiercely. I turned, and headed towards the cafeteria.

Here it was, our last breakfast together. I grabbed a tray and filled a plate, then went to the coffee machine. I walked towards our table, and only Sandy was there. I hadn't spent too much time with her this week, and I was happy to have some one-on-one time.

As I was walking up, Sandy spoke to me.

"Have you ever thought of changing your name?"

It shocked me, and I said, "well, no, not really."

"All week, I've been thinking that your name doesn't fit you. Cindy seems like a little girl."

I laughed, and thought back on the memory I just had of little Cindy in an Easter dress.

"Funny you should say that. I was just thinking about being a little girl, and my mom dressing me up so girly. It never felt like me."

She laughed, "Cindy makes me think of Cindy Brady. It's not you really. You need a name that's more serious - something short and powerful."

Her comment made me think of Cindy Lu Woo, from the *Grinch Who Stole Christmas*. I had friends in Ohio who called me by that name. I told Sandy that.

The whole conversation seemed odd, but also made me think about that little girl my mom used to dress up, Cindy. It wasn't me anymore.

Just then Diane walked up and said, "Cindy Brady, Cindy Lu Woo, what are you guys talking about?"

"Sandy thinks my name doesn't fit me," I said.

"Actually, it doesn't seem grown-up enough for you," Diane responded. "Are you going to change it?"

"I have no idea. I never thought about it until just now, but I think Sandy is right. I think I've outgrown my name."

"Yes, I can see you with a new name, and with longer hair!" said another woman, Ruth.

I laughed, and reached up to touch my hair.

"I've heard that from other people, about my hair. I guess it's time for some change!"

Suddenly I was aware of the attention, and began to feel uncomfortable so I diverted the attention in another direction. But inside I felt a current of energy, like the one I've been feeling all week. I knew that Sandy was right; my name didn't fit. It was time for me to let Cindy go and step into something new. But I had no idea what I would call myself. I'd have to give it some thought.

I quickly was absorbed back into the chatter of our last meal together. It was a madhouse of last conversations, goodbyes, and talk about keeping in touch. A few people got up to leave, needing to get to the airport for a flight, and we began giving hugs. It felt good to feel so connected, yet sad to be parting ways. I hugged everyone, said my farewells, and went to drop off my tray in the kitchen.

I walked to where my car was parked behind the Staffhouse. It had been nearly a week since I had been in the car, and it felt strange to get in and get buckled up. It was hard to believe it was time to go.

I sat there for a few minutes, getting settled in. I turned on my cell phone - no signal - and started the engine. I turned on to the narrow dirt road that headed out to the main road. I drove slowly, taking in the entire place as I drove. When I reached the entrance, I got out and took one last picture of the ranch, with an old wagon in the foreground.

This was it. I was leaving and I knew I had made the connection I had been yearning for, for decades. My heart swelled. My eyes filled with tears and I was overcome with emotions. This place had been calling me, New Mexico had been calling me, and I understood it now. The peacock talisman I drew from the bag the first night had been a true prediction of the week; it was about re-birth. I had had a re-birth here, and I was leaving a different person than the one who had arrived just a few days before. I feared that leaving would break the spell and I would be absorbed back into my life, all this forgotten. But another part of me knew that was impossible, what happened to me here I would never forget. I could never be the same. Yet, driving away was so hard. I forced myself to get back in the car. Looking in my rear-view mirror as I drove, I watched as the Ghost Ranch vanished from my view.

A Voice from Thin Air

"Hearing voices no one else can hear isn't a good sign, even in the wizarding world." - JK Rowling

It wasn't long before I was at the end of the dirt road and back on the two-lane highway heading to Santa Fe. Once I was on the pavement, I had a sense of letting go of the Ranch and the experience, and returning to the real world. I started to think about the day ahead and mentally plan what I wanted to do. Several women from the retreat had gone into Santa Fe on our free afternoon and found a bead shop. It sounded like a good one; I had asked the name, and decided I would head there as my first stop.

Santa Fe was about an hour-and-a-half drive, so I relaxed into driving, and enjoyed the view. This road was just as beautiful on the way out as it was on the way in, but now I was seeing it from a whole new perspective. I had a sense of knowing that I didn't before, and I felt part of this place. I took a deep breath, and just allowed myself to bask in the journey and the beauty in every direction. I knew that my real life was just a two-day drive ahead, and I was going to make the most of every minute of this journey home.

My mind started to wander, thinking back on the morning. The walk I took at sunrise, and the memory of my mom dressing me up, her "living doll." I thought about Sandy asking me if I had ever thought of changing my name. I felt exhilarated and alive with feelings, not sure what to make of the whole thing. A new name; what an interesting idea! I was processing it all and thinking about the possibility. But, what I would call myself?

My thoughts were all over the place as my body unconsciously navigated the car around the winding curves. It was interesting to even consider changing my name. What would it mean? Who would I be? It was so quiet, just me, in the car on the road. No other cars in sight. I was about five miles from the Ghost Ranch, out in the middle of nowhere. It was serene, peaceful, and vast. I was sitting in the driver's seat, but I felt like I was floating along the road.

Suddenly, from out of nowhere, the words "*Zia Poe*" floated into the car and into my ears. Or did it come from inside my head? I wasn't sure, but I heard it. It was as if someone spoke it quietly. *Zia Poe.* I felt an electrical charge run through my body (again), and I gasped. What was that? Where did that come from?

Zia Poe.

Zia Poe.

I repeated it several times. I felt tingly. Where had that name come from? It shocked me. Afraid that I would forget it, I slowed down, pulled over, grabbed a pad of paper and a pen, and wrote it down quickly.

Zia Poe.

I drove on.

Zia Poe.

Zia.

Zia Poe.

I repeated it again several times, the name ringing in my head.

Again, I asked myself, where did that come from? It felt like the words flowed like a warm breeze that just whooshed into the car. It was freaky, yet felt so real. It wasn't clear to me where the words came from; they just arrived out of the ether or out of the crevices of my unconscious mind. I had no idea. I drove along thinking about this name. Could I call myself Zia? And what about Poe? I wasn't sure I liked it. It reminded me of Edgar Allen Poe, and that seemed dark and kind of scary.

"Hello, my name is Zia, Zia Poe," I said out loud in the car.

Saying it out loud was a jolt. It felt foreign and peculiar, yet familiar in a bizarre way. What was going on? What am I thinking? Where did this name come from?

I said it again, "I am Zia. Zia Poe."

This time, I laughed out loud. What was going on? I had never heard the word Zia before; how could I think of that? And Poe - what a weird combination!

In my mind, I said the words Zia Poe. I repeated it over and over, considering the possibility of that being my name.

What was happening to me?

In a matter of seconds, this name appeared and I am freaked out, really thinking this could be my new name. What!?

Okay, this is too much, too strange. I paused. I convinced myself I better let it go and think about something else. I gave myself a little shake and brought my attention back to driving and the road ahead. That was just too weird.

I kept driving, but couldn't stop thinking about having a new name. I decided that I would make some up on my own.

I passed a sign that read, "okhay." That was an interesting name. Okhay. I considered it for a moment, and then realized that wasn't it.

Then, I saw the name Osuna on a mailbox. Zia Osuna? No, that wasn't right.

Then I tried a few others, Luna Malone, Tai Osuna, Zia Okhay. It seemed silly and difficult.

All the time, the name Zia Poe was glaring like a neon sign in my mind. That was "the" name. It had come so quickly, out of nowhere, like a message.

I was a bit freaked out and decided that I had spent too much time in the quiet, so I plugged in my iPhone and turned on some music. That is what I needed. "Lovely Day" by Bill Withers blared out of the speakers. Ah, yes, distraction.

*   *   *

Houses were beginning to dot the landscape, and I knew I was getting close to civilization. I checked my phone, and sure enough I had three bars. Santa Fe was just about 10 miles. I typed the name of the bead shop in my map app and got the directions. It wasn't far. Before long, I was back in the hustle and bustle of the city. It was raining slightly; I turned on my wipers. The streets were slick and shiny. Somehow, I missed a turn, and ended up on a one-way street. It took a while of re-routing, but I eventually found the store. Right next door was a coffee shop. I thought I'd go there afterwards. This was going to be fun.

It was a small little shop, and cases of beads lined the front and created islands around the store. This was going to take some time. I checked out every case and all the different containers of beads, charms and stones. They had a great selection. In another, smaller room, they had a gift shop with all kinds of stuff. I picked out a bunch of unique beads, a few cards, and a scarf.

I thought about the peacock that had become my symbol for the trip, and asked if they had any peacock charms. The clerk looked around and found a small gold peacock feather. I thanked her, but it wasn't at all what I was looking for.

Just then, a woman checking out at the counter pointed to the window and said, "There is a peacock."

I turned to look, and there was a tall, clear glass vase with a beautiful peacock in bright colors painted on it. It was stunning! It wasn't what I had in mind when I asked for a peacock charm, but it was magnificent. I knew I had to have it, and didn't even look at the price tag. My stomach did a little flip flop with excitement. This was the perfect souvenir. I took it off the shelf and brought all my treasures to the counter. The clerk wrapped the glass vase and put it in a box to keep it safe. She gathered my beads in small bags and prepared a little bundle for me. With a quick flash of my debit card and a signature, I was happily carrying my haul to the car. I got in, and then remembered the coffee shop next door. I hesitated for a minute, and then decided I didn't need any coffee. I should find the freeway and get on the road to Gallup; I had spent a lot of time here.

Since I didn't have a clue which direction the freeway was, I got out my phone again and mapped it. Before long, I was pulling out and heading towards the freeway. It was about seven miles, and I had to retrace a route that I had been on when I was here the week before. It all looked so familiar. A few blocks down the road I saw a cute, little coffee shop, one I had seen when I had stayed here. I passed it, and then realized I wanted to stop. I did want coffee, and I wanted to try this place.

I turned left onto another one-way street, and had to drive several blocks to find my way back. But, eventually I made my way to their parking lot. I went in the back entrance and walked up to the counter.

Behind the counter was a young woman barista; she was friendly and said, "Hi!"

I said, "Hi" back with a smile.

Just then I looked at the counter and there was a small white board that read, "Serving Today - Zia Blend." My heart skipped a beat. ZIA BLEND? What?

"What is that?" I asked her, pointing to the small white board.

"Oh, that," she grabbed the sign and erased Zia Blend and said, "that was the coffee we were serving this morning, but we're out."

I looked at her, the sound of Zia Blend echoing in my ears.

"That is so weird," I said in a whisper. "What is it?" I asked, thinking she would explain Zia to me.

"It's just a type of coffee. I'm sorry we don't have it, but I can make you something else."

She looked at me strangely, thinking I was disappointed.

"No, no. It's just that this morning I thought about changing my name, and the name that came to me was Zia," I blurted.

"Wow," she said. "Now, that's a sign!"

We both laughed. I stood there for a moment just looking at her.

She continued, "If you would have come in a few minutes later, there would have been a new coffee written on that board."

"Yeah," I acknowledged, but was dumbfounded.

If I had gone to the other coffee shop, I wouldn't have come here. And, if I hadn't turned around and come back here, I would never have seen this sign. Or, if I had been just a few minutes later, it wouldn't be here. How weird. It *was* a sign.

I ordered my coffee to go. I thanked the barista, and turned to leave.

She said, "Bye Zia, have a great day."

I smiled, laughed, and gave her a quick wave. I was beginning to feel like I was in an episode of the Twilight Zone.

Back in the car, my thoughts were whirling. What a weird coincidence! Zia. What was going on?

I started the car and found my way back towards the freeway. I passed the Sage Hotel where I had stayed the week before, and kept heading west. I couldn't stop thinking about the coffee sign and the how weird that was. It had to be real, this name that I heard in the car. It must be my new name.

What was the likelihood of that happening randomly? It wasn't possible. Was it?

At that moment, I realized the signal light in front of me was yellow and about to turn red. I became fully present, and slammed on the brakes.

Everything I had on the passenger seat went flying onto the floor. I was out too far in the intersection. I put the car in reverse, and backed up quickly. It shocked me. I had been so lost in thought that I nearly ran a red light. Well, I was alert now! While I waited for the light to change, and my heart to return to a normal pace, I reached down to pick up all the stuff on the floor. As I piled it back onto the front seat, I looked to the right. There was a train station and a huge sign that read "Zia Road Station."

My eyes nearly popped out of my head, and I felt that sudden rush of electricity run through my body, and my heart race again. Zia Road? What was going on? I had driven down this exact street several days ago, and had never seen that train station or that sign. This was crazy. I had never in my life heard the word Zia before this morning, and now I had seen two signs in less than 30 minutes. I was confused, excited, and shocked. I didn't know exactly what to feel. But I knew something strange was going on.

A beep of a horn brought me back to reality, and I realized the light had turned green. I took one last look at the sign, and stepped on the gas.

Zia Road. I wasn't quite sure what to make of it. It was too surreal to be just a coincidence. It was there for me to see. What if I had stepped on the gas and rushed through that light instead of stopping? I had stopped out of reaction, then backed up into a spot where I could see that sign. Yes, I had to admit it was meant to be seen. The whole thing seemed staged just for me. Both incidents. Two events as confirmation of the name I heard in the car. It was just too crazy.

Zia.

Zia Poe.

I said it out loud a few times. It was an interesting name, and I was beginning to like it. Part of me was still feeling I was in some bizarre alternate world, and another part of me felt it was just the continuance of the magical events of the past 10 days. Amazing. I was given a new name, and then I had it confirmed, or something. Is that what happened?

The freeway on-ramp appeared, I merged onto it, and I was on my way home. I was leaving Santa Fe behind, and it was about 280 miles to Gallup. There was a lot to process, and I wasn't sure what to think. I was happy to have all the miles between me and home to get my mind around the week at the Ghost Ranch and the events of the morning. I thought I should call someone and tell them what happened, but who? How could I explain it? I wanted to tell Sandy; she would get it. Actually, she would be surprised; who wouldn't? She had been the messenger; she brought the idea forward. Even that was meant to be. She and I alone this morning at the table.

Her first words to me were, "Have you ever thought about changing your name?"

Yes, I needed to tell her. I had to tell someone. But how could I reach her? I decided I could send a Facebook message to Chris and ask her to pass it on. That just might work. At the next off ramp, I got off, pulled over, found my phone, and sent Chris a message briefly explaining what happened and asking her to pass it on to Sandy.

Ah, that felt good. I told someone, I wrote it down, and it felt more real. They would get it; they would understand. They wouldn't think I was crazy. Or, was I? It didn't feel like it.

I imagined myself going home and telling people, "I was driving through the desert of New Mexico. Suddenly, I heard the name Zia Poe and knew it was meant to be my new name. Then I went to a coffee shop where they were serving Zia Blend, and then passed a train station at Zia Road. So, I knew it must be a sign."

Yeah, that made sense. Right. What was going on?

I needed a distraction. An audio book - yes, that was it. Fortunately, I had downloaded a few before I left and now seemed like the perfect time for a mindless guilty pleasure. I clicked on the Carrie Diaries by Candace Bushnell. Yes, the antics of a teenage Carrie Bradshaw would certainly get my mind off the mystical happenings in my life. Or at least it would be noise in the car.

Carrie did the job. A couple of hours later I was deeply involved with her budding affair with an older man she had met at a glamorous NYC publishing event, and her fear of telling him she was a virgin (the beginnings of Sex in the City), when I realized I was hungry.

There were signs along the freeway for restaurants at the next two exits, the town of Grants. Exiting at the first one, I spotted a small, clean-looking cafe. I went in, found a seat, ordered my lunch, and got out my iPad. Although I was listening to Carrie, my mind had still been on the whole Zia incident. I wanted to look it up and find out if it had any meaning. I settled in, sipped some iced tea, took a deep breath, and typed "Zia" in the browser. My heart was beating a bit faster as I waited for the search engine to do its job. It took a few seconds, and there it was. A list of items related to Zia.

The first thing my eye caught was an image. It was the symbol for New Mexico - a little circle with four lines coming out in four directions. I had seen it on the flag and on license plates. What? My head was spinning. The symbol for New Mexico is called a Zia? I never knew that symbol had a name.

I sat back and stared at the screen. I clicked the symbol, and it brought up a new window. The Zia sun symbol originally came from the Zia Pueblo, an indigenous people of the region of New Mexico. What?

It was happening again - that weird, otherworldly feeling. The name that came out of the air and I heard in my car was the name of the symbol that represents New Mexico, the name of a tribe of Native Americans? Zia.

How did I not know this? How come I had never heard this before, or knew the name? I wondered if the people in New Mexico knew it. Was it a common thing to know?

I wanted to ask someone in the restaurant, "Do you know what they call they little symbol on your license plate?"

I was dumbfounded, again. What does this mean? I read more and also found out that Zia represents harmony and balance in all things under the sun. The four lines in each direction represent the powers of nature, the directions, the seasons, phases of the day (morning, noon, evening, and night), and the stages of life (childhood, youth, adulthood, and old age). The Zia people also believe in the four sacred obligations - strong body, clear mind, pure spirit, and a devotion to the welfare of others.

My lunch arrived, and I kept reading more links. The power and meaning of this symbol was amazing. I wasn't sure what to think. Now it made sense why the coffee and the train station were called Zia.

When I finished eating, I turned off my iPad and just sat there looking around the restaurant. My mind was reviewing what I had just learned. The place was full of people, and I looked at a few of them and wondered about their stories. Did they live in this town or were they passing through like me? What was on their minds? Some looked happy and animated; others looked kind of sad. What would they think if they knew what had happened to me today?

I imagined standing up and saying, "Today I decided to change my name to Zia. Zia Poe! What do you think of that?"

Then I imagined they would all stop eating and just stare blankly at me, with a "who cares" kind of attitude.

Or maybe one person would start clapping, then the whole place would join in, and I would bow. Ha!

Then I switched it up, and imagined someone would say, "You can't call yourself Zia - that is the sacred symbol of New Mexico and the Zia people! Who do you think you are?"

Just then I noticed one man looking at me strangely, like he was reading my thoughts, I diverted my eyes quickly, looked down at my empty plate, moved around the iced tea glass, and put my napkin on the table.

Was I going nuts? It was time for me to get out of here!

CLAIMING ZIA

"Always speak your truth, even if your voice shakes." - Author Unknown

Back on the road, my mind was spinning reviewing the information I had just read. I wasn't quite sure what to make of it all. But, there was something about my connection to New Mexico and this entire experience that felt right. For decades, I had been drawn to this place; I felt it in my bones. There was something about New Mexico that called to me in a way I have never felt before about land. I had felt it at the Ghost Ranch, the deep stirring it created within me. It was something I couldn't ignore. Then this name Zia and how I heard it. Now that I was learning what it represented, I wasn't sure what to think. But, it was real. And it meant something.

There is no way all that had transpired in the past few hours had no meaning. This was big and powerful, and part of the transformation that began many days ago. Maybe it had been decades in the making. It hit me just how big this was. It was about me being transformed.

I thought of the peacock talisman I drew the first night at the retreat - the words "Protection surrounds you in this time of resurrection and rebirth" on the back.

This is it. This name and its meaning is part of my rebirth. I could feel it. There was no way to escape it.

By late afternoon, I had made it to Gallup. I checked in to my hotel, and then spent the rest of the afternoon shopping on old Route 66 in the famous pawnshops and bead stores. It was a nice distraction from the whole Zia thing. I loved looking at all the vintage turquoise jewelry. Looking at the cases and cases of jewelry brought me another sense of familiarity and connection. There was so much history in these cases. It felt more like a museum or art gallery. What an amazing tradition, and each piece so unique and different. The craftsmanship that went into each design.

Suddenly I realized that I was scanning the cases for a Zia symbol, any type of jewelry that had it incorporated. I couldn't find any, then asked the woman behind the counter.

When I asked for something with a Zia symbol she wasn't sure what I meant. I said, "You know, the sun symbol on the New Mexico flag."

She nodded, searched up and down the length of the cases, and only found a couple - one a bolo tie and a pair earrings. Neither interested me.

I thought it was interesting she didn't know the name Zia. She was from here. Maybe it wasn't commonly known.

Back at the hotel I knew it was time that I check back in with the real world, so I got out my phone. I was concerned how to respond to any questions about the retreat and my trip. How could I explain what had happened? It was a lot to tell. I contemplated it for a few minutes. Then I dialed my husband Jeff's number. I needed to tell someone I could trust.

He answered on the first ring.

I told him I was in Gallup, the retreat was over, and I was on my way home. He asked how it went, and I briefly described the painting and the Ghost Ranch. It would be impossible to explain all that had happened to me. But, I thought I'd tell him about the name thing.

"Something weird happened to me today, and I think I am going to change my name," I said tentatively.

"Really?" he questioned.

"Yes. The name is Zia. What do you think of that?" I breathed out quickly.

"Zia? Interesting."

"It was the strangest thing. This morning at breakfast someone asked me if I had ever thought of changing my name, and she thought Cindy was too young for me. Plus, earlier in the morning I had been walking and thinking about myself as a little girl and how she felt like an alien to me. Then I drove away, and a little way down the road the word Zia just appeared," I rambled.

"Appeared?" he asked.

"Well, not appeared, but came from somewhere. Like I never heard that word before and it just came out of the air and I heard it." I said, feeling like I was not making any sense. "Honestly, it felt like it whooshed into the car. Almost like someone spoke it."

"Well, that is weird."

"No kidding. But, the truth is, I think I have to do it. I think I was given this name because of all that happened, and who I am now isn't that little girl Cindy."

I then proceeded to tell him stories about the retreat, the paintings, and the Native American spirit that came to me at the journeying session. Then the two crazy sightings of the word Zia and finding out its meaning. It all just poured out of my mouth. This was the first time I had said this out loud, and it felt good.

"Wow. A lot happened. I like the name Zia. But, I think I will call you 'Z.' It reminds me of that cartoon I used to watch with the girls; you know the one, Moose A. Moose and Zee. Remember that?" he asked me, with a laugh.

I laughed too. I did remember. He used to watch that show with our granddaughters when they were tiny. They loved it, and so did he. This is what I liked most about my husband; I could tell him anything and he was supportive, accepting, and never judged me. What a gift.

"Yes, I do," I answered him. "You're funny. You can call me 'Z,' I'd like that." I smiled into the phone.

"Do you think the Native American spirit experience had anything to do with the name coming to you?" he said, now in a more serious tone.

I had thought of that too, and wasn't sure what to think.

"How so?" I asked him.

"Well, maybe it has something to do with why you always liked New Mexico and felt so drawn there. Maybe that spirit that came to you was from the Zia tribe. Maybe that is where the name came from."

"That crossed my mind too, but how could that be? It's just so out there. But, after everything that has happened to me in the past few days, I guess anything is possible," I answered.

The memory of the journeying workshop came into my mind, and I could vividly remember the experience. The figure, spirit, apparition, whatever it was that came to me seemed so real, and I felt so connected to it. Was it possible that he was the one that whispered the name Zia Poe in the car? That sounds crazy! But could it be? That would make sense in some ways. I had had a profound spiritual experience at the Ghost Ranch that included the journey. What if it were true?

"You're right; anything is possible. Don't you always say to keep an open mind?" Jeff reminded me.

"Yep, that's what I say. Actually, it's a quote from Wayne Dyer, 'Keep a mind that is open to everything and attached to nothing.' I try to live by that. But, this trip is testing me."

He laughed.

We talked some more, and then said our goodbyes.

I was exhausted, and the hotel bed was luxurious compared to the one at the Ghost Ranch. It had very soft, fluffy pillows and a down comforter. After a long, hot shower, I climbed into bed. Just as I was falling asleep, I remembered I hadn't told Jeff about the Poe part of the name.

The Final Straw (or Feather)

"The hardest challenge is to be yourself in a world where everyone is trying to make you be somebody else." - E. E. Cummings

The room was dark when I woke up. It was early. I lay there for a minute, mentally planning my day. I wanted to stop in Flagstaff for breakfast, but could I drive that far before eating? How far was it? How long would I have to drive today? I wanted to get home before dark. Home. Wow, I was going to be home today. Back into my real life. Back in the world of Cindy, and I didn't feel like Cindy anymore. That was going to be weird.

It felt sad; all this was going to be over, this adventure, all the magic, and not knowing what was going to happen next. I didn't want it to end, but I had to go back. Tonight, I would be home, back in my own bed. Tomorrow, I would check on my parents, see how they did while I was gone, and see what they needed from me. Jeff would have piled up the mail. I'd have to go grocery shopping, unpack, and start laundry. My life. Cindy's life. How could I hold on to this?

I took a big sigh, stretched, and closed my eyes. With closed eyes, I could connect to the bigger part of me, the part that easily connected to the oneness. I took a few deep, slow breaths and felt calmness encompass me. My mind cleared, my heart rate slowed, and I knew that all I had was this moment. There was no sense jumping ahead; just be present in the now. And that is exactly what I did. I lay in that state for a few minutes, then slowly got up and started the day.

It didn't take me long to get ready, pack the car, and get going. On the road, I continued listening to the audio book. It was a good way to pass the time and quiet my mind. Listening to the story of young Carrie was actually kind of fun, and I fantasized about what it would be like to be young, free, and living in New York City. She was just starting her life as a writer.

Then, I realized that when I was 17 I was writing too. I worked on the school newspaper; I had all through high school. I had a weekly column called "Rapping with the Rovers." My friend Debby and I would go around campus asking kids the question of the week, usually something provocative. It was great! Back then, I had dreamed of going to college and getting a degree in journalism and being a reporter.

I laughed out loud. That hadn't worked out, at all! It occurred to me that I was having a rebirth, and I could start new. Like Carrie, I could take my writing seriously and call myself a writer. Zia Poe was a writer! Again, I laughed out loud. A do-over at 58 years old. Was that possible?

I didn't have to go to college; I knew I could write. After all, I did have a book nearly completed that I had shelved out of shame and fear. I also had a children's book started. Yes, I could be like Carrie, only better. This was a do-over, and I had lots of wisdom to bring to my "new beginning." It felt exciting to think about. For so long, I had been trying to figure out what I was supposed to be doing. I had tried so many things, and abandoned so many paths. Writing was my first love and I had never stopped writing, but I just hadn't taken it seriously. Maybe it was time. Zia Poe the writer. Umm.

Then I said out loud, "My name is Zia Poe and I am a writer."

It sounded weird to hear my voice after so many miles just listening to the audio in the car.

I said it again, "My name is Zia Poe and I am a writer."

This time the Poe stood out, and I remembered I hadn't told Jeff about it in the conversation last night. Why? I thought about it for a few minutes. I didn't use his last name, so it wasn't that I was afraid it would insult him.

I realized I wasn't sure I really liked the "Poe" part of the name. Maybe I should just change my first name. That would be easier; people would understand that. But changing both first and last was big - maybe too big for me to deal with. Plus, Poe reminded me of Edgar Allen and it just felt a bit creepy, although he was a famous writer! It occurred to me that I hadn't looked up the meaning of Poe, and I decided I would look it up when I stopped for lunch. I pushed play on my iPad, and continued the audio book.

A few hours later, I stopped in Kingman, Arizona for lunch. I ordered and ate in silence, thinking about Carrie, writing, and taking the name Poe as mine. I finished eating and pushed the remains aside. I got out my laptop, connected to the Wi-Fi, and typed "Poe" in the browser. When the list came up, my eyes scrolled down the page. Suddenly, the word "peacock" jumped out at me.

WHAT?

My heart started to race in the eerie way it had been doing off and on the past couple of weeks, and I clicked on the link. The description came up.

POE;

This interesting and unusual surname is a variant of Peacock, which is of Anglo-Saxon origin. . .The nickname is derived from the Middle English (1200 - 1500) "pe, pa, po", peacock, from the Old English pre 7th Century "pea, pawa", and the Old Norse "pa"; these are derived from the Latin "pavo", the Middle English "cok", male bird, from the Old English "cocc", was added later.

Poe is a variant of the word peacock! Goosebumps spread over my arms, and that crazy jolt of electricity ran through my body. Poe comes from the word peacock. I could hardly believe my eyes.

I realized that I had stopped breathing, and took a deep breath. This was nearly impossible for me to believe. If I had felt like I was having strange experiences before, this topped them all. The name that had come out of thin air, while I was driving alone in the middle of the desert, had such significant meaning based on the past two weeks that it just blew me away. Zia, the symbol for the state of New Mexico and the Zia Pueblo, and now Poe, a variant of the word peacock. What the hell was going on? I sat there dumbfounded, yet again. I closed the lid of my laptop. I just stared off, my mind desperately trying to process this new information. Quickly, I tried to think of a rational explanation. Nothing. Poe, peacock. It was just so damn strange. Or, was it?

It was a long time before I moved. A sort of calm had come over me, an acceptance. There was no fighting or questioning what was going on. It was suddenly very clear to me. I gathered my stuff, and walked to the car. I got in, sat there for a little while, and let it all sink in. This was real; it was deeply real, and it was time I acknowledged it.

Eventually, I started the car and headed for Interstate 40. I was going home. If I had questioned the name before, I knew now that it was real. It was meant to be mine. When I saw that word peacock, I knew it; I had all the confirmation I needed.

Nearly two weeks earlier I had started this adventure to New Mexico as Cindy Eubanks, but I knew, without a doubt, that today Zia Poe was on her way home.

Epilogue

"The secret of change is to focus all of your energy, not on fighting the old, but on building the new." - Socrates

The first two weeks home were hard. I had changed, but the people and situations in my life had not. I moved through my days in a fog, trying to assimilate what I had learned and how I had changed, back with my "normal" life.

But my life wasn't normal any longer.

First, I knew I had to write this story. It was some internal drive that I couldn't hold back. Plus, I wanted to reflect on what happened so I could remember it all and also verify my own sanity. Thankfully, I had my handwritten journal, the one I wrote in every day on the trip, my sketches, and my laptop files. I also had photos to remind me of events and the beauty of the land. All this helped me keep the story fresh, and the events in order.

I returned home from New Mexico in September, and I started writing my story on November 1st. I was even telling the story in my sleep, and would wake up and write. It flowed like water.

In December, I had surgery on my throat at UCLA Medical Center. The surgery had a few complications, but ended well.

The doctor removed the tumor, and there was no permanent damage to my vocal cords. I did have slight nerve damage, but very minor. The tumor was benign, as expected, and I began to feel better within days. It seemed that my throat crisis was over.

But, my life crisis was not.

I had lived without boundaries and outwardly focused for so long, the people in my life were well trained. Changing things at this point was going to be a challenge. However, it was a challenge I had to face; I had no choice. I knew I could no longer live as Cindy. Although I felt like Zia, the world had a hard time accepting it. It took a while for me to ease into telling people. Some were supportive and excited about the adventure I took.

Others, like my mother, reacted very badly. She refused to even talk with me about it. The conversation brought up a host of other issues, and exploded into some hidden truths being revealed. My mother had been holding in feelings for years about me not taking my husband's last name, and decided now would be a good time to tell me. Honestly, I was shocked at her reaction. I had lived as "Cindy Eubanks" for a long time - years! I had decided long ago not to take my husband's name. I had no idea this bothered her.

She looked at me sternly and said, "I'm embarrassed and ashamed of you for not using Jeff's name! It is an insult to him, and I can't believe you are so selfish!"

She was furious and nearly in tears.

I looked at her, astonished.

"Mom, this is something I decided a long time ago. Jeff and I talked about it. He is perfectly okay with it."

"He wouldn't tell you if he was!" she responded with sarcasm.

Just then, Jeff spoke up. He'd been sitting on the sidelines quietly.

"That's not true. I agree with her. Why does a man keep his name for life, and a woman has to take her husband's name? I am perfectly okay with it."

"Well, I'm not! And I think this conversation is over!" she said firmly.

It seemed this moment of real, honest communication was finished.

That was the end of any conversation about my name. By the next afternoon things had returned to normal with her, like nothing ever happened.

Most of the rest of my family and friends accepted the change, although I don't think they fully understood why I changed it. Another reason I wanted to write the story.

I decided I wouldn't legally change my name until after my mom passed away, out of respect for her. But I changed it almost everywhere else, and began to live as Zia.

Over the next few months, I knew I had to make some changes. Once I had this awakening, I couldn't ignore it any longer. First, I had to get out of the high desert. I had made a mistake moving there. It was the place I lived my entire childhood, and we were living less than a mile from my childhood home. These were not pleasant memories. This place reminded me of the trauma and the isolation I'd felt as a kid. I hated the wind, the desert, and the tumbleweeds. It was like going back to live near a war zone. Living near my mom, who had created her own altered reality about our childhood and the desert, didn't help one bit.

Then, there was my marriage. We had grown apart years ago, and were living two separate lives. We were friends, and we loved each other. But there was no romance or passion, and no shared vision for our life. We'd been separated before, and this time when we got back together I had promised myself we would make it work. And, we were. He did his thing, and I did mine. We were even sleeping in separate rooms. Now, I realized this wasn't enough. It was settling, and it wasn't right. I knew I had big changes to make, and it was going to be very, very difficult. But, I also knew I didn't have a choice.

In my office/bedroom I set up a meditation area. I decided that I would start my mornings with some time to connect to my higher self by doing some meditation and journaling. As the days passed, it was becoming more and more clear what I needed to do. During the meditation time, I was clearing my mind. Then I would write, and the wisdom poured out. The fear was huge and intense. I knew that what I had decided would disrupt the lives of people I loved. That was something I'd spent my life trying to avoid. Be a good person, fill their needs, and then they would love me. Wrong. That is exactly what I learned becoming Zia. That is what led to the tumor in my throat. So, I knew that I would have to hurt or disappoint them (or whatever feeling it caused them), but it couldn't be helped.

I'd decided that I wasn't ready to make a final decision about my next step, but I was ready for "Part B" as I called it. I would go stay in Bellevue, Washington for eight to 10 weeks, away from the desert, my parents, and Jeff, and decide what "Part A" was going to be. Part A would be the big jump; Part B would be the little one, but enough separation that I would be able to think things through and decide on my future. The most important part was being honest with them and clearing the air.

First, I talked with Jeff. He wasn't surprised. He knew I was unhappy and that we had been living more out of convenience and habit than anything else. We had a deep connection, but it wasn't romantic - it was something else. I didn't want to lose that, but I knew living without feeling loved was not something I could continue. He wasn't happy with the news, but he understood. I told him I would be leaving for at least eight weeks, staying with our daughter. She had a private bedroom and bath that was designated mine, so it would be a good place to get away. I'd decided I would leave in three weeks.

Next, I had to tell my parents. After a lot of thought, I decided the best thing for them was to move into an independent living building - a place that fixed their food and cleaned their apartment. They had wanted to do this a couple years ago, but then changed their minds. I thought this was the perfect time to re-visit that option. The place they looked at before had openings. I visited, and found two nice apartments for them to look at. My brother was coming for the week, and I thought this would be the best time for me to talk with them and take them to visit the place. And that's what we did.

The hard part was explaining it to them. I had to let them know how unhappy I was in the desert, with my marriage, and that I needed space and time to figure out what I was going to do next. It felt like I was abandoning them, but I knew the place we picked out would offer all they needed and would be better for them in the long run. They had lots of questions, but surprisingly they understood, too.

The relief I felt is indescribable. I'd managed to tell my husband and my parents that I couldn't put their needs before mine any longer, and I had to take care of myself. That was big, HUGE! This was something I never dreamed I could do, that I would never have the nerve to do, but I did it. What I learned about myself at the Ghost Ranch was truth so real that I couldn't possibly ever go back to being the way I was before.

Once the decision was made and I had been honest with everyone, I started making plans. I wrote lists of things I needed to do, made arrangements with the facility, made plans with movers for my parents, and started gathering boxes to pack what I was taking with me. There was a lot to do in a short period of time. It was a crazy, busy, emotional, and exciting time.

On the morning of September 1, 2014, I was up early, made coffee, and went to my meditation chair for my morning practice. Jeff had gone bicycle riding with his friends for their normal Monday morning ride. It was a beautiful morning, and I settled in for my 20-minute meditation.

About halfway through my cell phone rang, and I decided to ignore it. A few minutes later the home phone rang. I ignored it. A few minutes later my cell phone rang again, and I turned it off.

Of course, I had lost my meditative state and my mind starting spinning.

"What if something happened to Mom or Donny? I better call them. No, it can wait 10 minutes! Finish your meditation!" I remember thinking.

Then my phone made the sound it makes when someone leaves a message. The distraction was too much. I looked at my phone and the missed call was from Jeff. I hit the voicemail button with a sigh, thinking he probably had a flat, but the voice on the message was not his.

"This is the San Bernardino County Sheriff's Department; your husband has been in an accident, and I need you to call back as soon as possible."

To say my heart skipped a beat is an understatement. The adrenaline rush made me lightheaded. I pushed the call button on my phone, and a paramedic answered on the first ring.

"Hello," he said.

"This is Jeff's wife. Is he okay?" I said breathlessly.

"No ma'am, he's not. He was knocked unconscious and we're having some difficulty bringing him around. We are taking him to St. Mary's Hospital. Can you meet us there?"

"Yes, I'm leaving now."

I hung up, rushed to get dressed, and got in the car. I headed to the hospital as fast as I could. I arrived within 15 minutes.

When I was finally allowed into to see him, I could see it wasn't good. He had scrapes and was a bit bloody; he had on a neck brace, and was hooked up to all kinds of tubes. He smiled when he saw me.

"Hey," I said. "The things some people do to get attention!"

He smiled again. He wasn't speaking, and looked really out of it.

The nurse said the doctor would come talk to me shortly.

Jeff closed his eyes. I covered him with a blanket, and waited.

It didn't take long. The doctor came in and said that Jeff had suffered a brain injury and had bleeding on the brain. He also had broken his jaw in three places, and they were worried about spinal injury. He told me that St. Mary's wasn't equipped to deal with these types of injuries, so they had contacted the nearest Brain Trauma Center and Jeff was going by Life Flight helicopter. Time was of the essence. They couldn't wait to send him by ambulance.

The doctor leaned down by Jeff and loudly said, "Mr. Cochran."

Jeff opened his eyes, and looked confused.

"You had a bike crash and suffered a head injury. We are going to have to send you by helicopter to another hospital," the doctor said.

Jeff just stared at him.

"Can you tell me what day it is?" the doctor asked.

Jeff shook his head, no.

"Can you tell me who this woman is?" the doctor said, and pointed towards me.

"My wife," Jeff answered in a very weak voice.

"Good, can you tell me who the President is?"

Jeff looked a bit dazed, and then replied, "Obama, but I didn't vote for him."

The doctor and I both laughed, and it was the first moment that I thought he might be okay. But those were the only two questions he could answer. Everything else the doctor asked him was jumbled or he didn't know the answer. Where he lived, what state we were in, what month, nothing.

The doctor looked at me.

"Okay, the Life Flight should be here any minute. They will be taking him to Arrowhead Hospital in Colton. It's about an hour away, driving. You won't be able to go with him, so you'll have to drive. Is there anyone you want to call?"

I nodded my head, "I need to call our kids."

"You go do that, and we'll get you when they arrive," he said in a comforting way.

Just then, one of Jeff's bike buddies arrived and we went out in the hall. He told me what happened. They were riding in a pace line. The guy in front of Jeff slowed down and Jeff hit his tire, but no one saw what happened next because they were all facing forward. All they heard was him hitting the ground. By the time they stopped and looked back, he was lying on the ground unconscious. He said there were going about 20 miles per hour when it happened. They called 911, and the paramedics arrived within five minutes.

I just stared at him, not sure what to say or think. What a freak accident! I asked more questions, and he told me all he could. I asked if he could stay with Jeff, and I went to make calls.

A few minutes later, the helicopter team arrived - a doctor and two nurses. Within seconds, it seemed, they had him strapped up and ready to fly. They talked to him constantly and hooked him up to portable machines. I kissed his cheek, and told him I would be there as soon as I could. He was rolled off to the awaiting helicopter, and I headed to the parking lot. I was just about to the car, when I heard the sound of the helicopter taking off. I looked up and watched as Jeff was flown away.

Two days later, the bleeding on his brain had stopped. The good news was no brain surgery. But, his jaw was another issue. An oral surgeon came in to explain the damage. His jaw was broken in three places - the ball joint had popped out on his right side and broken off. It was a very difficult break and there was no guarantee that surgery could fix it, but it was the only option. However, if we did go the surgery route his mouth would be wired for weeks. She felt the brain injury issue was more critical, and that jaw surgery didn't seem like a good decision at this time. She told me to think about it, and she'd come back later.

The brain surgeon and his team came into his room, and described to us what happened. The bleeding on the brain caused a Traumatic Brain Injury. The bleeding had stopped, and that was a good sign. There was no spinal injury, and aside from a few scrapes and road rash, his body was in good shape.

The main concern now, was seizures. It was common, or at least not uncommon, for people with brain injuries to suffer seizures. There was also no way of knowing how much damage was done to his brain, or the after effects. He said it would be a matter of time. A brain injury like Jeff's is similar to a stroke. He said we needed to start physical therapy and see what happened.

It was clear that Jeff wasn't his old self. He couldn't walk straight, had major balance issues, his memory was pretty much gone, and he was mixing up things in his head and looked confused most of the time. When the doctor came back and said they were releasing him, I was stunned. He said to follow up in a week, and also call Jeff's primary physician and make an appointment. Then he walked out.

That was it. I sat there looking at Jeff. He was looking back at me, like a little child. I hadn't slept much in the last 48 hours; I was a mess. Jeff had been given medication to prevent seizures, so he was loopy. I couldn't believe he was being discharged! What in the hell was I supposed to do?

Plan C: Post Ghost Ranch, Year Three

"If 'Plan A' doesn't work. The alphabet has 26 more letters.
Stay Cool." - Anonymous

It's impossible to believe that over three years have passed since my crazy, wonderful, adventure to New Mexico. It's been over two years since Jeff's accident. Life is different - not at all what I had planned. I had not contemplated a Plan C!

Since the minute Jeff had his accident, and even to this day, something came over me; I call it compassion. But it is bigger than that. It was impossible for me not to understand that Jeff's bizarre accident that Labor Day was meant to be. Not necessarily for me to understand, but I know it happened for a reason. Obviously, I didn't leave and work on my Part B or Part A. That, along with working on this book, was set aside.

I moved even more into a caretaker role than before, but my feelings about it changed. This compassion I felt was so strong and so complete that I never once questioned why. Nor did I ever feel resentment towards him or the situation. The biggest part of me was filled with love and compassion for him, and I knew that I was in for the long haul. No doubt. I feel blessed for that.

What did happen is we moved. We sold our home in the desert and moved 90 miles away into a 700-square-foot, vintage, mid-century, singlewide mobile home in Palm Springs. It is amazing. I completely had it remodeled, and it is perfect for us. Palm Springs is fantastic! Living here is a joy, and it is so beautiful. Plus, there is so much to do. I couldn't be happier!

My parents moved into the independent living apartment, and they seemed to enjoy it. They had all the help they needed, lots of activities, and three meals a day prepared. My stepdad passed away in 2015. We moved my mom closer to us, and she lived another year. She loved living in Palm Springs. She passed away in 2016.

Jeff goes three days a week to the Neuro Vitality Center, a place that specializes in treating people with TBIs and strokes. He has made great strides, but will never be the same. He has memory, comprehension, and balance issues. I tell people he's like a 15-year-old boy. He has a happy disposition; he loves watching movies and eating sweets. We have figured out a way of life that works for us, and I'm at peace with it all.

It didn't come easily, however. The first few months after Jeff's accident were tough. Lots of appointments at the VA, which was an hour's drive each way. Physical therapy, TBI classes, dentist visits; it was crazy. All while I was helping my parents move, and getting rid of all their belongings they didn't take with them. Basically, 90 years of stuff, and lots of it!

Plus, Jeff could no longer do yard work or any of the work around the house he used to do, so that was on me too. I had to hire a gardener and housekeeper, just to stay sane, which didn't work! I realized we needed some place smaller to live, and that's when I found the mobile home. We sold our house and moved to Palm Springs. Moving was a huge chore and downsizing was crazy, but good. Then came the remodeling process, and driving back to the desert to help my parents twice a week. It was so much; too much! It broke me.

About a year ago, I was sitting on the couch watching TV. I felt relaxed; I had on my pajamas and was engrossed in a show. Suddenly, I had a feeling like nothing I had felt before, a rush of blood to my head, and then my heart started to race incredibly fast. It was so frightening that I didn't hesitate for a second; I picked up my phone and called 911.

I hung up and told Jeff, "Please stay calm. Something is wrong with me, and I need the paramedics. I called them, and they will be here any minute."

He looked stunned. I could hear the sirens in the background.

After a frightening evening at the hospital, they found no stroke, no heart attack. I was suffering from major anxiety, debilitating anxiety. It felt like a stroke or heart attack, but that was a common symptom in people with anxiety.

They referred me to my primary physician who then referred me for outpatient mental health treatment, TM (transcendental meditation), and prescribed Lorazepam. I signed up for a TM workshop. I started seeing a therapist and psychiatrist. I started weekly sessions with the therapist. I was diagnosed with anxiety disorder, post-traumatic stress disorder, and social anxiety. My therapist explained to me that this was just like any kind of illness, but it was mental. There was no shame or blame. I just needed medication and treatment.

Amazingly, this was the final piece of the puzzle. I knew I had something going on with anxiety, as I wrote about it a lot while I was in New Mexico, but it never occurred to me it was something that was diagnosable or treatable. I hated being labeled with "mental illness," but I knew it was true and it was real. After a few months of TM, therapy, and medication I felt like a new person. I had a comfort inside that I'd never had. It took a while, but was well worth the struggle. Now, I am stable and no longer in therapy. My meds are balanced, and I see the doctor every three months just to check in.

I've decided to be Zia Poe Eubanks, and keep my last name for the sake of genealogy. All the experiences I had in New Mexico, my tumor, Jeff's accident, my parents' deaths, and my breakdown have all contributed to my wholeness. The things I learned about myself while Becoming Zia are firmly assimilated into who I am today. I have owned them and embrace them, including my name. I am at last, at peace and comfortable in my own skin.

The journey to Becoming Zia may have been just two weeks, but living as Zia is a lifetime. I know there are more lessons to be learned and adventures ahead, but I approach them with a new understanding and excitement. I am no longer broken; I no longer need to be fixed. Being whole and accepting myself fully is the greatest gift of all.

LESSONS FOR EVERYONE

"The most valuable lessons aren't taught. They're experienced."

I came away from this experience with new knowledge and a deeper understanding of some big truths. I'd like to share them with you.

What Other People Think of You is None of Your Business!

This is life changing. You have NO control over what other people think! Absolutely none! You can't get inside someone's mind and insert thoughts. Oh, you can try. But, that is a giant waste of time. Spending any time worrying about, "what will people think" is squandering valuable energy. Accepting this fact is liberating! I encourage you to try it!

Growing up with my mom's mantra, "what will people think," as my behavior model did so much damage to me. This was her issue, not mine. But she spilled it on me, thinking she was protecting me in some way. Learning that I cannot control what people think of me or how they feel about me is a profound realization. It has changed how I feel about myself and how I interact with other people.

We Are in Total Control of Our Own Happiness!

Your level of satisfaction in your life is totally in your control. You are happy because you are having a thought about being happy. You are sad because you are having a thought about being sad. This works for all emotions - anger, frustration, envy, jealousy, etc. They all start with a thought. And guess what? You are in charge of your thoughts! I'm not saying you may need to make changes in your life, but the one thing you have complete and absolute control over is your thoughts about it. It's your choice. Really! When I finally got this, it changed my life. It could seriously change yours, too!

Many people have read the book "The Secret" and try to use those principles to manifest *things* into their lives. The real secret is that your thoughts create feelings, and the feelings bring things into your life. Every day you create your world by the thoughts you think. Every time you think a thought something in your life is being created. Why not deliberately choose your thought by starting with how you want to feel? It is one of our most important human gifts. There is no person or situation responsible for your unhappiness or happiness. It's all you!

Setting Boundaries is About Me, Not the Other Person!

For decades, I hung on to resentment like a badge of honor. It felt like if I let it go, the other person would be let off the hook. Then one day I had a new thought, and it knocked me for a loop. What if the reason I am so resentful is because I didn't set a boundary and stick to it? I let people walk all over me, because I had no boundaries. Then I resented them for taking advantage of me. This was not about them. I was holding on to the resentment because I was afraid to face the truth, that I had let myself be taken advantage of and be abused. Without standing up for myself or setting a boundary and committing to it, I had allowed myself to be hurt, and that felt terrible. Having a boundary means I respect myself. Me. Not forcing the other person to do what I want them to do. No, it's about self-respect and not being willing to tolerate situations or behaviors that diminish me on any level. Now, that's self-esteem! When I realized this, I knew I was on my way to real health. Setting boundaries took on a whole new meaning.

Mental Illness is Real, and Nothing to Be Ashamed About!

There is no denying I was suffering from a mental health issue.

When I was sitting in the ER, and the doctor asked me "Are you under a lot of stress?" - I knew.

I had been carrying the weight of the world on my shoulders as a caretaker of three people, plus all the logistics of moving my parents, us, Jeff's rehabilitation, the remodel, etc. I'd exceeded my maximum capacity. But what I didn't realize then, but did after weeks of therapy, was that I had been suffering from this since childhood. I had just developed coping mechanisms to deal with it. I had learned to compensate and adjust, until I couldn't anymore. There is no shame in that. It is an illness. An illness that went untreated my entire life.

There are so many people in the same situation - dealing with anxiety, depression, or PTSD. The world looks at that as a "troubled person." But, it is an illness that happens to humans when they've been emotionally damaged. I encourage anyone who thinks they might have this issue to seek help. I'm no doctor, but I've lived it, and know there is help for you!

#1 Lesson I Learned - You and Your Life are Perfect Just as They Are!

I spent the better part of my life trying to "fix myself" because of what I called "being fucked up." It was because of my childhood issues, crazy PTSD father, narcissistic, self-absorbed mother, living isolated in the desert, having a "bunker" as a home, etc. Then there was the sexual abuse, drug and alcohol addiction, my weight issues (oh yes, my weight issues!), being physically abused for years by my first husband, social anxiety, etc. Yes, I had deemed myself one giant mess. I could go on and on!

But, you know what? I'm not fucked up! Nope, never have been. This life of mine - it's been perfect. You know how I know that? Because this has been *my* life. It *is* perfect. It's exactly the life I am supposed to live and the experiences I am supposed to have.

I am part of the greater whole. Yes, that woo, woo stuff. But, it's true and real. Whatever that is (God, the Universe, the Force), I am a piece of that. And, whatever that is, I am. That means I am love, acceptance, compassion, abundance, and everything that the greater whole is. I am a unique expression of the divine, and so are you. We all are. That is what being human means. And being human means you get to make choices and do stupid things, and have good things happen and bad things happen. It's called life! It's so awesome. So, how can I be fucked up? I can't.

Accepting this truth, the biggest truth, is what changes everything and brings a sense of peace like nothing else. It's not about religion. It's bigger than that. It's a oneness that connects everything and everyone. When you change the way you look at things, the things you look at change. Accepting that I had and am having the perfect life is letting go in a big way. And, learning that lesson is the best gift ever!!

What I hope for you, my reader.

First, I want to thank you for making it this far in the book and hanging in there with me! This book has been a cathartic experience for me, one that I needed to share. Lots of crazy stuff happened to me along the way and I promise you it's all true. Some of it may sound very weird and out there; at times I thought so myself, and questioned my own sanity.

But, I'm a regular woman living a regular life and happened into something mysterious and magical. Yes, I told you I was diagnosed with mental illness, but I did not hallucinate any of this. My mental illness is anxiety-related. So, trust me when I say this is a true story!

What I hope you take away is the lessons I learned. When it gets boiled down, it clearly comes to some basic truths, which I wrote about above. I want you to read those over again and learn from my wacky, bizarre journey. These are truths that can change your life.

Whatever the reason all this happened to me, I know that I was driven to share it from a powerful place. Something inside me wouldn't allow me to let go or give up. Soon it will be four years since I left the Ghost Ranch, but the lessons are fresh and the truth still stands strong!

Thanks for reading about my journey. I hope you find some piece of this that speaks to you and helps you in some way.

I've decided to write a workbook to accompany this book for those of you who want to work on your own journey. I'm calling it *Becoming You! An Interactive Workbook*. It will be a guide through the lessons and the discoveries I had along my journey. If you want to delve into your own personal discovery, I encourage you to check it out. You can find it on Amazon. It became the logical next step in my process.

I've discovered that the something in me that wants to be expressed is about knowing people and myself on a real authentic level. There is nothing more gratifying then really connecting with another person. I've shared the real me here, and I hope that by doing that I may help someone else know their own self just a little bit better. That would be so wonderful!

In wholeness and with grace,

Zia

ABOUT THE AUTHOR

Zia Poe Eubanks

Zia's creativity has always been her driving force. Since she was a young girl making dolls, she has turned to art as a means of self-expression. She started writing in her teens, and has learned to use writing as a way to process her life. She has also been blogging for years.

Throughout her life she has been a teacher and coach - teaching art, consciousness, and principles of the Law of Attraction. Zia is currently working on several writing projects and developing a program based on the lessons she learned while on this journey.

She lives with her husband Jeff in Palm Springs, California. She also spends time in the Seattle area with her daughter and her family. She is a member of the Palm Springs Writers Guild and the Pacific Northwest Writers Association.

She has written a companion book to *Becoming Zia* called *Becoming You! An Interactive Workbook*. It is a tool to explore some of the lessons from the book. It is available on Amazon.

You can find out more about her at www.ziapoe.com

Here is Zia's Amazon.com Author Page:
www.amazon.com/Zia-Poe-Eubanks/e/B073X887BQ

Here's something you can do for me!

If you enjoyed *Becoming Zia*, I'd appreciate you leaving a review on Amazon. It is simple to do by going to the book on Amazon and click on "leave a review." The more reviews I get, the more people who will be able to enjoy my book because it will rise in the ranking. Thank you for taking your time to support my writing.

RESOURCES

Thanks to these wonderful women for guiding me through this journey!

- Painting from the Wild Heart Retreat, Chris Zydel
  www.creativejuicesarts.com

- The Life Coach School, Brooke Castillo (Check out Podcasts and Self Coaching Scholars)
  www.thelifecoachschool.com

- Be Your Own Beloved, Vivienne McMaster
  www.viviennemcmasterphotography.com

- Wear Your Joy Project, Kellie Rae Roberts
  www.kellyraeroberts.com/wear-your-joy/

- One Little Word, Ali Edwards
  www.aliedwards.com

www.ingramcontent.com/pod-product-compliance
Lightning Source LLC
Chambersburg PA
CBHW031620040426
42452CB00007B/595